GOD'S NAME, GOD'S NATURE

GOD'S NAME, GOD'S NATURE

VICTOR BOOKS®

A DIVISION OF SCRIPTURE PRESS PUBLICATIONS INC.
USA CANADA ENGLAND

Recommended Dewey Decimal Classification: 221.8
Suggested Subject Heading: BIBLE, O.T.–GOD'S ATTRIBUTES

Library of Congress Catalog Card Number: 88-60206
ISBN: 0-89693-584-1

VICTOR BOOKS
A division of SP Publications, Inc.
            Wheaton, Illinois 60187

•CONTENTS•

•INTRODUCTION•

God's name unlocks the mystery of His nature, reveals His heart, mind, and soul, captures our imagination and brings us to His feet in wonder, love, and praise. To study the names of God will bring us closer to heaven and make us pleasanter people to live with. Enjoy His names as you discover Him through this book.

•BEFORE YOU BEGIN•

People who gather together for Bible study are likely to be at different places in their spiritual lives, and their study materials should be flexible enough to meet their different needs. This book is designed to be used as a Bible study guide for such groups in homes or churches. It can also be used by individuals who are studying on their own. The lessons are written in five distinct sections, so that they can be used in a variety of situations. Groups and individuals alike can choose to use the elements they find most useful in the order they find most beneficial.

These studies will help you learn some new truths from the Bible as well as how to dig out those truths. You will learn not only *what* the Bible says, but how to use Scripture to deepen your relationship with Jesus Christ by obeying it and applying it in daily living. These studies will also provide an opportunity for potential leaders to learn how to lead a discussion in a nonthreatening setting.

What You'll Need

For each study you will need a Bible and this Bible study guide. You might also want to have a notebook in which to record your thoughts and discoveries from your personal study and group meetings. A notebook could also be used to record prayer requests from the group.

The Sections

Food for Thought. This is a devotional narrative that introduces the topic, person, or passage featured in the lesson. There are several ways it can be used. Each person could read it before coming to the group meeting, and someone could briefly summarize it at the beginning. It could be read silently by each person at the beginning of the session, or it could be read aloud, by one or several group members. (Suggested time: 10 minutes)

Talking It Over. This section contains discussion questions to help you review what you learned in Food for Thought. There are also questions to help you apply the narrative's truths to daily life. The person who leads the discussion of these questions need not be a trained or experienced teacher. All that is needed is someone to keep things moving and facilitate group interaction. (Suggested time: 30 minutes)

Praying It Through. This is a list of suggestions for prayer based on the lesson. You may want to use all the suggestions or eliminate some in order to leave more time for personal sharing and prayer requests. (Suggested time: 20 minutes)

Digging Deeper. The questions in this section are also related to the passage, topic, or character from the lesson. But they will not always be limited to the exact passage or character from Food for Thought. Passages and characters from both the Old and New Testaments will appear in this section, in order to show how God has worked through *all* of history in people's lives. These questions will require a little more thinking and some digging into Scripture, as well as some use of Bible study tools. Participants will be stretched as they become experienced in the "how-tos" of Bible study. (Suggested time: 45 minutes)

Tool Chest. The Tool Chest contains a description of a specific type of Bible study help and includes an explanation of how it is used. An example of the tool is given, and an example of it or excerpt from it is usually included in the Digging Deeper study.

The Bible study helps in the Tool Chest can be purchased by anyone who desires to build a basic library of Bible study reference books and other tools. They would also be good additions to a church library. Some are reasonably inexpensive, but others are quite expensive. A few may be available in your local library or in a seminary or college library. A group might decide to purchase one tool during each series and build a corporate tool chest for all the members of the group to use. You can never be too young a Christian to begin to master Bible study helps, nor can you be too old to learn new methods of rightly dividing the Word of truth.

Options for Group Use
Different groups, made up of people at diverse stages of spiritual growth, will want to use the elements in this book in different ways. Here are a few suggestions to get you started, but be creative and sensitive to your group's needs.

☐ Spend 5-15 minutes at the beginning of the group time introducing yourselves and having group members answer an icebreaker question. (Sample icebreaker questions are included under Tips for Leaders.)

☐ Extend the prayer time to include sharing of prayer requests, praise items, or things group members have learned recently in their times of personal Bible study.

☐ The leader could choose questions for discussion from the Digging Deeper section based on whether participants have prepared ahead of time or not.

☐ The entire group could break into smaller groups to allow different groups to use different sections. (The smaller groups could move to other rooms in the home or church where you are meeting.)

Tips for Leaders
Preparation
1. Pray for the Holy Spirit's guidance as you study, that you will be equipped to teach the lesson and make it appealing and applicable.

2. Read through the entire lesson and any Bible passages or verses that are mentioned. Answer all the questions.

3. Become familiar enough with the lesson that, if time in the group is running out, you know which questions could most easily be left out.

4. Gather all the items you will need for the study: name tags, extra pens, extra Bibles.

The Meeting
1. Start and end on time.

2. Have everyone wear a name tag until group members know one another's names.

3. Have each person introduce himself or herself, or ask regular

God's Name, God's Nature

attenders to introduce guests.

4. For each meeting, pick an icebreaker question or another activity to help group members get to know one another better.

5. Use any good ideas to make everyone feel comfortable.

The Discussion

1. Ask the questions, but try to let the group answer. Don't be afraid of silence. Reword the question if it is unclear to the group or answer it yourself to clarify.

2. Encourage everyone to participate. If someone is shy ask that person to answer an opinion question or another nonthreatening question. If someone tends to monopolize the discussion, thank that person for his or her contribution and ask if someone else has anything he or she would like to add. (Or ask that person to make the coffee!)

3. If someone gives an incorrect answer, don't bluntly or tactlessly tell him or her so. If it is partly right, reinforce that. Ask if anyone else has any thoughts on the subject. (Disagree agreeably!)

4. Avoid tangents. If someone is getting off the subject, ask that person how his or her point relates to the lesson.

5. Don't feel threatened if someone asks a question you can't answer. Tell the person you don't know but will find out before the next meeting—then be sure to find out! Or ask if someone would like to research and present the answer at the group's next meeting.

Icebreaker Questions

The purpose of these icebreaker questions is to help the people in your group get to know one another over the course of the study. The questions you use when your group members don't know one another very well should be very general and nonthreatening. As time goes on, your questions can become more focused and specific. Always give group members the option of passing if they think a question is too personal.

What do you like to do for fun?
What is your favorite season? dessert? book?
What would be your ideal vacation?
What exciting thing happened to you this week?
What was the most memorable thing you did with your family when you were a child?
What one word best describes the way you feel today?
Tell three things you are thankful for.

10

Imagine that your house is on fire. What three things would you try to take with you on your way out?

If you were granted one wish, what would it be?

What experience of your past would you most enjoy reliving?

What quality do you most appreciate in a friend?

What is your pet peeve?

What is something you are learning to do or trying to get better at?

What is your greatest hope?

What is your greatest fear?

What one thing would you like to change about yourself?

What has been the greatest accomplishment of your life?

What has been the greatest disappointment of your life?

Need More Help?

Here is a list of books that contain helpful information on leading discussions and working in groups:

> *How to Lead Small Group Bible Studies* (NavPress, 1982).
> *Creative Bible Learning for Adults*, Monroe Marlowe and Bobbie Reed (Regal, 1977).
> *Getting Together*, Em Griffin (InterVarsity Press, 1982).
> *Good Things Come in Small Groups* (InterVarsity Press, 1985).

One Last Thought

This book is a tool you can use whether you have one or one hundred people who want to study the Bible and whether you have one or no teachers. Don't wait for a brilliant Bible study leader to appear—most such teachers acquired their skills by starting with a book like this and learning as they went along. Torrey said, "The best way to begin, is to begin." Happy beginnings!

1
Elohim

•FOOD FOR THOUGHT•

"What is the chief end of man?" a catechism teacher asked a young boy. The boy replied, "The chief end of man is to glorify God and 'endure' Him forever." Of course he meant "enjoy"—I think! Some teenagers and parents too, for that matter, believe that to glorify God must surely mean they would have to "endure" the religious consequences of such an occupation. Before I knew the Lord in reality, I secretly believed that God would so spoil my fun, I would never smile again! Quite frankly though, the knowledge of God is not the chief end of too many men!

People have interests so many other directions than Godward. For many it is football or some other sport. For others the chief end of their Mondays are Fridays and weekend partying. Still others put all their energies into raising children and homemaking. This is not to say all these ends or goals are not good things, but they should not be the chief ends of our lives.

The knowledge of God enables us to honor Him and the more we know Him the better we love Him. The knowledge of God is an eternal thing of everlasting benefit. Jesus Himself said, "Now this is eternal life: that they may know You, the only true God, and Jesus Christ, whom You have sent" (John 17:3). To know Him is to live forever to enjoy Him.

There are many ways we can study God in order that we might know Him. When we read the Gospel account of the life of Jesus Christ, we see God in the flesh. Jesus was God in Galilean cloth. He was "the exact representation of His being" (Heb. 1:3). Or we can look at His creation and see Him reflected there. Then we can come to know God as we see Him in the lives of those who have accepted Him. The only problem with learning about God from His creation or His creatures is that both are spoiled by sin and give us a less-than-perfect picture.

We can study the written Word of God that reveals the God we should glorify, or we can study His names. The Hebrews laid great store by names. They believed names showed character. Therefore, the names of God became a medium of revelation for the Hebrew people. Jesus Christ said, "I manifested Thy name to the men whom Thou gavest Me out of the world" (John 17:6, NASB). And again, "I have made Thy name known to them, and will make it known" (John 17:26, NASB).

No one name can fully or adequately express God's fullness. Each one we study will bring out a special virtue. The second king of Israel was called David, for example. He could also have been called Shepherd, Giant Killer, Warrior, King, Prophet, Poet, or Musician. If so many names are necessary to describe a man, how much more the Lord? God knew that if He was going to reveal Himself, He must use many names, each of which would tell us something of His glory.

The first name we will look at is **Elohim** (pronounced El-Lo-Heem). This Hebrew word for God is found over 2,000 times in the Old Testament. It is the only name of God found in Genesis 1. It is in this first chapter of the Bible that we are introduced to the mystery of the divine substance. The very words and the way they are used in the Hebrew language teach us aspects of God's character.

El, one of the most used terms for deity known to the human race, is a plural noun, and the name given in Scripture most often to describe the Trinity is Elohim. We are readied right from the start of Creation for the mystery of a plurality in God: "Then God said, 'Let Us make man in Our image, in Our likeness' " (Gen. 1:26). In other places, a singular noun is used, teaching us that this Elohim, though plural, is but one God. In fact, in some instances, both are used in one sentence. For example, Isaiah heard God asking, "Whom shall I send? And who will go for Us?" (Isa. 6:8)

Even though the Trinity may remain a mystery to us, we can try to understand why God chose to tell us He is three in One. After all, He didn't need to tell us but He did; so we can presume there is information in that piece of revelation from which we can benefit. As we see the Trinity in action through the Bible, we learn that there is unity between the members of the Godhead. There is a divine harmony of purpose and operation in creation. In Genesis 1 it is God, Elohim, who speaks the word and sets the stars spinning, the mountains quaking, and the birds singing. But don't forget the Spirit who hovered or brooded over the waters, helping to make it happen. And hear the Apostle John say, "In the beginning was the Word, and the Word was with God, and the Word was God. He was with God in the beginning. Through Him all things were made; without Him nothing was made that has been made" (John 1:1-3).

The Trinity seems to be at work also in the Incarnation. Gabriel came from God to tell Mary that the Spirit would impart the Christ to her womb. But it is in the baptism of Jesus that we see the three members of the Godhead most clearly. Jesus, the Son of God, came out of the water and the Holy Spirit in the symbolic shape of a dove rested on Him, while God leaned out of heaven to tell us, "You are My Son, whom I love; with You I am well pleased" (Luke 3:22).

Elohim is derived from the verb **alah** which means to swear and describes one who stands in a promised covenant relationship ratified by an oath. This derivation reveals yet another aspect of God's person to us—God has sworn to be faithful. He is under the obligation of that oath. It is unthinkable to believe that having sworn to do something He would renege on His promise.

So what has God sworn to do? To be faithful to His promise to be faithful! To whom? First, to Himself. God is totally committed to Himself in divine eternal unity and faithfulness forever. In other words, He has a certain relationship in and with Himself which, because He is God, can never be broken. Jesus spoke of the love He enjoyed in bygone ages before He ever became a baby in Bethlehem. "And now, Father, glorify Me in Your presence with the glory I had with You before the world began. . . . Father, I want those You have given Me to be with Me where I am, and to see My glory, the glory You have given Me because You loved Me before the creation of the world" (John 17:5, 24). In his book *Names of God* (Kregel Publications), Andrew Jukes quotes St. Augustine: "If God is love, then in God there must be a Lover, a Beloved, and the Spirit of love, for there can be no love without a lover and a beloved!" The relationship in God, in and with Himself, is one in which there can be no breach. From the beginning, God is Elohim in covenant union with Himself!

Second, God has sworn to be faithful to His creation. Other ideas that come from this name are Sovereign, Creator, and Omnipotent. In Genesis 1:1-24, Elohim is used 35 times. Some believe that there is a period of time, or a gap, which exists between the events described in Genesis 1:1 and 1:2. They maintain that God created the heavens and the earth, but that Satan fell and, consequently, the world became "formless and empty." This view is supported by Isaiah's statement in 14:17 that God did not create the world "formless and empty." If God did not create it like that, then it must have become like that after Satan's fall. God has sworn to restore His spoiled creation until it is all *very good* again. Though part of creation was "formless and empty" with darkness over "the surface of the deep" (Gen. 1:1), Elohim did not forsake it. When nothing else moves, the Spirit does! Surely the sensible thing would be to scrap the spoiled world and start all over again. But God has promised to perfect His creation till there is in the end "a new heaven and a new earth" (Rev. 21:1).

Genesis reveals a God who can't rest until His fallen creation is restored and re-created. Some believe the debris we read about in Genesis 1:2 was all that was left of the once beautiful kingdom of Satan and his angels who had destroyed the earth. In God's promise to Noah, we hear Elohim promising never to destroy His creation by flood again. In fact, He promises restoration with the same oath as He promises Himself unity.

The third thing God wants us to know about Himself is that He is similarly committed to the creature of His creation. The theme of the Old Testament is covenant! Noah looked up and saw a rainbow, the colors of which would remind him of the promises of God on his behalf. Noah had a wonderful opportunity to start all over again. He had a new life in a new world and, I'm sure, a new awareness of the grace of God. It is incredible, therefore, to see him lying in a drunken stupor in his tent soon after this new opportunity (Gen. 9:21). Man's heart of sin seems to be incapable of loving God, glorifying God, and enjoying Him forever! The sad record continued. Man rebelled and made his gods from sticks and stones, stars and constellations, and ended up worshiping the creature more than the Creator.

But Elohim did not wipe man off the face of the earth. He had promised to restore him. Yet Israel continued to live in the midst of men and women who served their own elohims. Many unbelievers in the God of Abraham, Isaac, and Jacob were very religious, serving many gods. To distinguish the God of Israel as supreme from others of the class elohim, certain appellations were added to His name. **El Elyon** designates the God of Israel as the *highest* among the elohim. The word could be used as the highest of a tier of baskets, or of a nation above all other nations, or as the being higher than all other beings. It was the heathen King Nebuchadnezzar who came to recognize God as El Elyon saying, "At the end of that time, I, Nebuchadnezzar, raised my eyes toward heaven, and my sanity was restored. Then I praised the Most High; I honored and glorified Him who lives forever. His dominion is an eternal dominion; His kingdom endures from generation to generation. All the peoples of the earth are regarded as nothing. He does as He pleases with the powers of heaven and the peoples of the earth. No one can hold back His hand or say to Him: 'What have You done?' " (Dan. 4:34-35)

The Israelites also understood that El Elyon, being the highest God among gods, had the prerogative of drawing the boundary lines around His people's dwelling places and the sovereign power to designate their land and their inheritance.

Not long ago we bought a lovely home on a lake with an inheritance from my parents. The day we moved in, I read: "Lord, You have assigned me my portion and my cup; You have made my lot secure. The boundary lines have fallen for me in pleasant places; surely I have a delightful inheritance" (Ps. 16:5-6). El Elyon had been as good and as true as His name!

Another revelation of God's character is hidden in the name **El Olam**—the everlasting God. He is the "age" God or the God of the ages. He is working out His ultimate purpose through the ages, revealing His hidden agenda to the person who will seek His will and cooperate in that venture with Him.

El Ro'i means *the God who sees*. Hagar discovered He is the living God who sees our plight (Gen. 16:13). She came to believe that God was not standing in the shadows with His hands in His pockets!

El Shaddai, translated by the English words, *God Almighty*, explains to us that God, who is the God of nature, has the power to compel that same nature to do what is contrary to itself. It is a name that reveals God as especially able to bring life into deadness. Abraham came to understand what El Shaddai could do despite the law of nature where childlessness was concerned. The root idea of this name gives us the idea of "the breast"—the nourisher or supplier of needs, the satisfier of the thirsty soul—the God who is sufficient.

This particular aspect of God has an especially tender place in my heart. If indeed He is the God who is enough, then I do not need more than an Elohim who answers all my needs. He will nourish and satisfy me whether or not I have a husband to help me, children to love me, or health to sustain me. In my past, present, and in my future, I know El Shaddai will be all that I need, as the occasion arises.

How can I be so sure? Because His names reveal His Person, and I have come to know Him, honor Him, and enjoy Him—and He has promised me I will do that forever!

•TALKING IT OVER•

1. REVIEW AND DISCUSS.   *5 minutes*
   - [ ] What is the chief end of man?
   - [ ] What does the name Elohim tell us about God in:
     Genesis 1:26
     Isaiah 6:8
   - [ ] In what great acts of deity do we see the Trinity in action?

2. DISCUSS IN TWOS.   *8 minutes*
   In twos, study each passage and identify which part each member of the Godhead plays in the incident.

Creation	Incarnation	Baptism	Crucifixion
Gen. 1:1	Luke 1:35	John 1:32	Heb. 9:14

3. READ AND RESPOND.   *7 minutes*
   Read Luke 17. What does Jesus teach us about His relationship in the Godhead from this chapter?

4. REFLECT AND SHARE.   *10 minutes*
   What aspects of God's character do the following names bring to mind?
   - [ ] El Elyon,   Genesis 14:18-20
                          Isaiah 14:14

   Read Daniel 4.
   - [ ] El Olam,   Genesis 21:10, 22-23
   - [ ] El Ro'i,   Genesis 16:13
   - [ ] El Shaddai,   Exodus 6:3
                         Genesis 17:1-2
                         Hebrews 11:11
                         Genesis 49:24

   Share how God has proved Himself to you through one of these aspects.

•PRAYING IT THROUGH•

Suggested Times

1. (As a group) Praise God for all the things He is: *5 minutes*
   □ To Himself.
   □ To His creation.
   □ To His creatures.
   Read Genesis 1 to yourself, then praise God for an aspect of creation that you particularly appreciate.

2. (On your own) Confess your sins and weaknesses.   *3 minutes*
   Thank Him for His promise of forgiveness and restoration. Remember that the name Elohim reminds us of God's faithfulness. Thank Him silently for a promise that He has kept.

3. (As a group) Pray for people who: *8 minutes*
   □ Serve Elohims of their own making!
   □ Fail to look beyond immediate circumstances to remember God is El Olam, God of the big picture.
   □ Like Hagar need to believe God is El Ro'i, the God who sees our needs.
   □ Need to be reassured that God will supply their needs because He is El Shaddai, the God who nourishes us.

4. (On your own) Meditate on and respond to one of   *4 minutes*
   the passages studied in this session, such as Genesis 1.

•DIGGING DEEPER•

Elohim (Gen. 1:1-31)

1. Read Genesis 1 and note the following observations:

   Repetition

   Contrast

   Cause and Effect Relationships

   Comparison

2. What does the opening statement of the Bible reveal about God? Why does the Bible not begin with how God came into existence?

   What does Genesis 1:2 affirm about the Spirit's activity in creation?

   By what means did God choose to create?

3. Is there any suggestion of disorder or struggle in the creation account? What does this suggest about God's nature? How can knowing this be of encouragement to you personally?

4. How does God view His creation? How must He feel about you then?

5. List the different phrases repeated in Genesis 1 and the number of times they recur. What is the significance of these repeating words, phrases, or ideas?

6. Find the two benedictions in this chapter by God on His creation. Identify their similarities and dissimilarities. What does your study show about the prominence of man in creation?

7. What does it mean to be created in the image of God?

   What are the moral, social, and spiritual implications of this truth for day-to-day life?

   Are both men and women created in God's image? Support your answer with Scripture.

8. Define the responsibilities man and woman were given when they were created. Do we still have the same God-given responsibilities today? Explain.

9. List all the evidences for the Trinity in Genesis 1.

   Record an illustration from everyday life that describes our three-in-one God.

10. Why would God choose Elohim as the first name by which to communicate His identity to man?

    What knowledge of God would you have if Genesis 1 were the only written revelation of Him available to you?

11. We often send our dear friends notes of appreciation not only for what they have done, but for who they are. Below, jot a note of appreciation to God, your Elohim.

For Further Study
1. Make a list of the days of creation and what occurred on each. Then memorize your list.
2. Check out *Themes in Old Testament Theology* by William Dyrness (InterVarsity Press) from a nearby Christian library or bookstore and enjoy reading pages 41–75.

•TOOL CHEST•
(A Suggested Optional Resource)

THEMES IN OLD TESTAMENT THEOLOGY

An enthralling tool, William Dyrness' *Themes in Old Testament Theology* (InterVarsity Press) helps systematize for us many Old Testament concepts, laying a firm foundation for our understanding of God and His purposes. Dyrness ties together the vast and sometimes overwhelming biblical material by tracing the development of each of the following themes:

1. The Self-Revelation of God
2. The Nature of God
3. Creation and Providence
4. Man and Woman
5. Sin
6. The Covenant
7. The Law
8. Worship
9. Piety
10. Ethics
11. Wisdom
12. The Spirit of God
13. Prophecy
14. The Hope of Israel

2
Adonai

•FOOD FOR THOUGHT•

God uses His names as a medium of the revelation of His character. They are intended to be a source of theological content for us. As we come across God's names in the Bible we should ask, "What does this name tell us about God?" Let's examine the name **Adonai,** translated by the English word **Lord.** It is not to be confused with the same English word LORD spelled with capital letters, meaning Jehovah.

When Abraham sat in the door of his tent and became aware of three men approaching him, he addressed them as "my Lord" or "Adonai" (Gen. 18:3). Apparently he was aware that the "men" represented God in human form. In fact, he had no doubt regarding the nature of their divinity, as the text of chapter 18 shows.

The word **adonai** was in general use in Abraham's day, and was used to describe an earthly "master." It was also used when a wife addressed her husband—as Sarah used it in Genesis 18:12, calling Abraham her adonai.

So the name adonai expressed a personal relationship which involved the rights of lordship and possession. Slaves and women in Abraham's day were "not their own." Both voluntarily or involuntarily they belonged to and were the property of their "lord."

Slaves were purchased with money, captured in war, or had been born to slaves already belonging to a master. Wives were either given or sold to men by their fathers. There might well have been an element of free choice in the transaction of the wife, as in the case of Rebekah, whose father asked her, "Will you go with this man?" (Gen. 24:58) But once the decision had been made, both a slave and woman lived in subjection to his or her lord or Adonai. God wanted to tell us that a relationship exists like this between God in heaven and man on earth. He constantly uses these titles, that of master and husband, as a picture of His relationship to us. God wants us to know He has a claim upon man's obedience and service.

Look at the story in Genesis 18. Abraham, well used to being called "Adonai," ran to Sarah and told her to make a special meal for their visitors. He helped with the preparations himself, and after serving the visitors, Abraham took the "servant's" place while they ate. Abraham's eyes were ever watchful for their needs, his ear in tune for any comment that came his way.

We are intended to wait upon our Heavenly Master in such a fashion—not out of fear, but out of love! In Hebrew law, provision was made for slaves to go free in the year of Jubilee. If for some reason a slave did not want his freedom, he could tell his master. The master would then take the slave to the marketplace where he would bore his ear through with an awl. Thus the loving, willing slave would be saying, "I love my master and my wife and children and do not want to go free" (Ex. 21:5).

Now he was earmarked, carrying in his body an unmistakable witness to his commitment and servitude. To be marked out in such a way would say much to those who saw that pierced ear! It would speak of a very special relationship between that particular master and his slave!

We who are Christians are expected to respond to our Adonai Christ with such service that we too will be marked men and women. What a challenge! Jesus Himself told us not to lord it over those we are responsible for but to serve God and our fellowmen humbly. Was it not Jesus Himself, after washing His disciples' feet, the lowliest service a slave could render, who said, "You call Me 'Teacher' and 'Lord,' and rightly so, for that is what I am. Now that I, your Lord and Teacher, have washed your feet, you also should wash one another's feet" (John 13:13-14).

Like Abraham, those of us with leadership roles must learn to serve our Adonai and our fellowmen, even as our Heavenly Adonai served us while here on earth.

Another obvious lesson we can draw from the master/slave analogy is that of unquestioning obedience. Slavery and obedience go together. When Isaiah looked through the door of heaven, he saw the Lord, "Adonai," sitting on His throne. He also saw the angels of God flying this way and that, ready to be obedient to God's commands. Then he heard the voice of Adonai asking, "Whom shall I send? And who will go for Us?" Isaiah responded with the words, "Here am I. Send me!" (Isa. 6:8) It was this aspect of the master/slave relationship that Isaiah had in mind when he addressed God, and this undoubtedly helped him to be obedient to the heavenly vision and continue his ministry among the same obstinate, backsliding people he had been serving for years. When his Master asks who will go, the willing, loving slave responds, "Here am I. Send me!"

It was Jeremiah's Adonai that told His scared servant to not be terrified by the people, but see to it that he delivered His message (Jer. 1:17). I have often found myself in Jeremiah's sandals. I have been scared of the hostile face of an offended churchgoer, an angry teenager, or an upset neighbor. Faces can be frightening things to face! At these times it has been the concept of Adonai, my Master, that has resulted in my obedience.

But if it is the concept of the master and slave that helps us to be obedient, it is the idea of the husband and wife relationship that softens His commands. The Old Testament is full of comments by our Heavenly Adonai to this effect. Isaiah says, "For your Maker is your Husband" (54:5), and "As a bridegroom rejoices over his bride, so will your God rejoice over you" (62:5). God reminds Jeremiah, "I was a husband to them" (Jer. 31:32). Ezekiel gives us God's allegory of Israel as an unfaithful wife and we hear God complaining, "You adulterous wife! You prefer strangers to your own husband!" (Ezek. 16:32)

Our heavenly Adonai expects us to be faithful to our marriage covenant with Him, honoring Him with all our heart, soul, mind, and strength! This picture is displayed in the New Testament where Christ is pictured as the Bridegroom with the church as His bride (Eph. 5:31-32). God wants us to grasp the idea that it should be as unthinkable for us to love the world as it would be to cheat on our spouses. We are to submit to each other with loving, responsive hearts.

How should this concept affect my life? The idea of service was born in my heart from the day I became a Christian. Just as the slave had no rights, only responsibilities, I too accepted that fact. Like the Old Testament slave, my time, money, service, and choices were my Master's, not mine. The master would even choose the slave's marriage partner and I determined He would choose mine. I decided I would try to listen for His voice and as best I could, run swiftly to do the things He told me to do. I underlined the commands in my Bible with a blue crayon so my eye would easily be caught by my Adonai's orders. I would search for these words in the morning, and in the evening ask myself the questions: "Did I obey Him? If not, why not?"

I read that God wants us to be honest servants, so I tried to tell people I had lied to them (if I had) and asked them to forgive me. I discovered that my Adonai wanted me to tell others about Him, so I endeavored to do that every day, simply sharing the things I was learning myself with a friend, family member, or even an enemy! I made no major decisions without first inquiring what my Master's wishes were. And so, from my earliest days as a believer, I learned obedience.

This was hard because slavery is not an occupation for weak-willed people. But I was helped along by the thought that my Adonai was not only my Lord and I His servant, but He was my "husband" and I, His "wife." He loved me and had shown me the full extent of His love by dying for me on the cross. I could be sure that the things He asked me to do were things in my very best interests.

I was never more aware of this aspect of my relationship with God than when my earthly husband was away from home for long periods of time. I do not sleep very well when Stuart is away. The house seems to be full of creaks and groans. I remember in the early years of our marriage, asking my "Heavenly Husband" to care for me while my earthly husband was out of town. I specifically prayed He would help me to sleep as soundly when Stuart was away as when he was home. *If God is my Husband*, I thought, *then He will give me that sense of security that makes it easy to fall asleep!*

I remember standing by the side of my bed struggling against my fears. Would I look under the bed, or wouldn't I? I knew that I wouldn't if Stuart were home. I managed to get myself in between the bed sheets without succumbing, but found myself lying as stiff as a board waiting to be murdered! I switched on the light (I hadn't wanted to put it off in the first place) and reached for my Bible. After a few minutes, I discovered this verse: "Indeed, He who watches over Israel will neither slumber nor sleep" (Ps. 121:4). "O Adonai," I whispered, "please look after me." I seemed to hear Him cheerfully say, "I will. Go to sleep now. There is no use in both of us staying awake!" And I went to sleep—yes I did!

What victory, and all because He showed me who He was and what He would do for me. As our Adonai, our Master, He had sent Stuart to do His business on earth, and He had given me my own work orders in his absence. As our Adonai-Husband, He assured Stuart and me of His love and dealt tenderly with our needs while we were apart. The Lord wants us to know He is as powerful and true as His great and glorious name!

•TALKING IT OVER•

---

1. REVIEW.
   Read Genesis 18:1-33. Note the different uses of the words **Lord** and **LORD**.
   ☐ What struck you about the aspect of God's character revealed in the name **Adonai?**
   ☐ Servant and master?
   ☐ Husband and wife?
   Which picture touched you most and why?

10 minutes

---

2. READ.
   Read Psalm 77:7-11 and Genesis 49:22-25. See if you can substitute the Hebrew names of God for the English translation.

10 minutes

---

3. REMIND YOURSELF.
   Remind yourself of the following aspects of God's character that need to play a more important part in your life.
   ☐ A caring master who gives you work to do.
   ☐ A loving husband who appreciates your love.

5 minutes

---

4. SHARE.
   Fill in the acrostic below with words or sentences that capture the meaning of lordship (A–Authority). Then share your acrostic, thanking God for each aspect.
   A
   D
   O
   N
   A
   I

5 minutes

•PRAYING IT THROUGH•

Suggested Times

---

1. (As a group) Read Isaiah 6:1-6. Praise God for the different apsects of the glory of Adonai Lord you see in this passage.

5 minutes

---

2. (On your own) Pray for:
   □ Your relationship with Adonai Lord, as servant and spouse.
   □ Your relationship with Jehovah as your Redeemer.

5 minutes

---

3. (As a group) Pray for:
   □ Others to know these aspects of God's character.
   □ The rebellious who need to be obedient and the lost who need to be saved.

3 minutes

---

4. (As a group) Pray for God's servants in the church:
   □ Pastors
   □ Elders or deacons
   □ Sunday School teachers
   □ Youth leaders
   Pray for new believers discovering their love relationship with God.

5 minutes

---

5. (On your own) Return to Isaiah 6:1-6. Fix your mind on the pictures in this passage and enjoy them!

2 minutes

•DIGGING DEEPER•

Adonai (Gen. 18:1-15)

1. Read Genesis 18:1-8. Observe Abraham's responses to the presence of the Lord in his life.

   How did the Lord's presence affect Abraham's behavior? What was he doing before the visitors appeared compared to after their arrival?

   Record the verbs describing his actions.

2. Abraham's flurry of activity mirrored what about his heart?

   Describe Abraham's offering to his Adonai.

3. Read Genesis 18:9-15. Where was Sarah during the Lord's visit, and what was she doing there?

   What does her answer in verse 15 hint about how she was feeling? What does it reveal about her character? Had the Lord addressed her? Why do you think she spoke up?

4. If you had been Sarah, why would you have needed to hear the Lord say, "Is anything too hard for the Lord?" (v. 14)

5. What did the Lord do with Sarah's lie?

Was the Lord truly Lord of Sarah's life? In which area(s) of her life did she need to experience His Lordship?

6. Are you more like Abraham or Sarah when it comes to acknowledging God's Lordship in your life? Ask God to help you identify where you need to trust in His loving husbandry. Now ask Him to help you surrender that part of you that has yet to come under His mastery.

7. Read Genesis 18:16-33 and 19:12-29. What evidences of the master/slave analogy do you notice in these passages?

What evidences do you find of the Lord's loving husbandry in these passages?

How can you apply these analogies to your own life?

For Further Study
1. Use a Bible dictionary to study Sodom. Look up the Scripture references. Was Adonai a harsh master toward the city's inhabitants? Defend your answer with Scripture.
2. Reread Ezekiel 16:49-50. If you are guilty of any of these sins, confess them to your Master and ask for His forgiveness.

•TOOL CHEST•
(A Suggested Optional Resource)

BIBLE DICTIONARY
An exhaustive Bible dictionary should be a constant companion for the student of Scripture. Keep it near your fingertips when studying or preparing a lesson to insure its use. This delightful tool opens the door of discovery to the world and times of the Bible. It is easy to use for it is organized just like our English dictionaries. Contained within its content are definitions, historical background, maps, diagrams, pictures, references, and explanations of the numerous entries. A thorough Bible dictionary is worth the investment but if cost is prohibitive a compact paperback is a worthwhile substitute. Listed below are a few for your consideration:

> *Harper's Bible Dictionary* (Harper & Row)
> *International Standard Bible Encyclopedia* (Eerdmans)
> *Interpreter's Dictionary of the Bible* (Abingdon Press)
> *The New Bible Dictionary* (Tyndale)
> *The New Compact Bible Dictionary* (Zondervan)
> *Wycliffe Bible Encyclopedia* (Moody)
> *The Zondervan Pictorial Encyclopedia of the Bible* (Zondervan)

3
Jehovah-Jireh

•FOOD FOR THOUGHT•

When God gave Jacob a vision of a ladder extending from earth to heaven, Jacob could not fully grasp the meaning of it. Lying under the desert stars, Jacob dreamed that He saw Elohim—a transcendent being—the One who existed outside the physical universe (Gen. 28:10-15). In contrast, the name **Jehovah** speaks of that aspect of God's character that is personal rather than transcendent. It is His personal name. God is reachable because He has chosen to be reachable. In fact, He reached out to man, descending the ladder from the highest heaven to the depth of our poor hearts. And so, the name **Jehovah** emphasizes the relationship of God to man and, more particularly, the relationship of man to Israel.

The *King James Version* of the Bible translates **Jehovah** with the English word LORD, using capital letters to distinguish it from Adonai-Lord. The name is used over 6,000 times in the Old Testament. Since Jehovah is first referred to in Genesis 2:4, there is no question that the patriarchs knew and used the name Jehovah, though its full significance was not revealed to them.

Moses was first to have the meaning of **Jehovah** fully explained to him. Moses busily argued with God about his suitability for the task God wanted to give him: "Suppose I go to the Israelites and say to them, 'The God of your fathers has sent me to you,' and they ask me, 'What is His name?' Then what shall I tell them?" (Ex. 3:13) God quickly responded to Moses. "I AM WHO I AM. This is what you are to say to the Israelites: 'I AM has sent me to you' " (Ex. 3:14).

Moses reluctantly went back to Pharaoh but found himself under terrific personal pressure. Had he heard God right? Would he indeed deliver the Israelites from bondage? God again encouraged Moses, assuring him it was not His will to leave His people serving Pharaoh. God Himself would become personally involved and bring the Isra-

34

elites out of Egypt. That is what Jehovah is all about. It can mean "I am what I am," "I will be what I will be," "I am here for you," or "I will be there as I am here!" Over and over again the Lord assured His people in Egypt that He had heard their prayers and had come to deliver them from their trouble. Jehovah is the name of redemption!

Jehovah also has to do with a covenant and a promise to a people. When we come to the Passover (Ex. 12:1-30), Jehovah is used 12 times. The Lord was telling man He is a personal, living being, fulfilling for the people of Israel the promises made to their fathers. He is, as His name suggests, an unchanging God. He cannot become better, because He is perfect. He cannot deteriorate for the very same reason. Nor can He renege on the promise He has made to Himself, His creation, and the fallen creatures in it—to mend that which is broken.

Another concept involved in the name Jehovah is that of revelation. God is a revealer, not a concealer. The name reveals that God is first a God of righteousness. The hints are there as early as the story of Cain and Abel, who offered sacrifices for their sins. At least Abel seemed to understand that God was indeed a God of "rightness" and he, being a creature of "wrongness," needed to say he was sorry for his sins (Gen. 4:4-6).

The hint of God's righteousness is in the story of Noah as well. Two creatures of every kind with the power to create a new being were drawn to the ark where Noah took them in. Noah was also instructed to take on board seven clean creatures of many types to use as sacrifices.

Jehovah, the Holy God, wants us to know He is deeply offended by sin—my sin, your sin, and the sin of the whole world! Because He is a God of righteousness, He has to do the right thing and judge our unrighteousness. Having judged it, He has to tell us we are guilty and deserve to die.

But Jehovah is not only a God of righteousness and holiness; He is also a God of love! It was this love that led Him to offer Himself as a substitute for our sin. "God was reconciling the world to Himself in Christ, not counting men's sins against them" (2 Cor. 5:19).

The compound names of Jehovah are names that are used in connection with places and incidents as in the case of Jehovah-Jireh. When God wanted to make a special revelation of Himself, as meeting human need, He used the name Jehovah. The faithful of Israel, fully understanding this special relationship that was theirs, cried often, "O LORD our God," or "Jehovah, Thou art our Elohim"

(2 Chron. 14:11). The godly Israelite knew that the two great attributes associated with Jehovah were righteousness and holiness. The very name Jehovah became so holy that men would not even pronounce it lest they be accused of blasphemy and put to death (Lev. 24:16). Even today the name Jehovah is never used in a Jewish synagogue. The name Adonai is substituted.

So the compound names owe something of their significance to the name Jehovah itself. Through the revelation of His names, men already knew that God was the eternal self-existent One, the God of revelation and moral and spiritual attributes—holiness, righteousness, and love.

Most of the compound names portray Jehovah in some aspect of His character as meeting human need. Genesis 22 describes the biggest crisis of Abraham's life. God had revealed to Abraham that he would have a son and through him and his descendants, all the nations of the earth would be blessed (Gen. 12:2-3). The great hope had been realized when El Shaddai overruled the laws of nature, and Sarah conceived when she was past age. Isaac was born, and Abraham and Sarah looked forward in faith to the historical fulfillment of God's promises through the centuries yet to come.

But now the crisis had to be faced! God appeared to Abraham and told him to offer Isaac, his only son, as a burnt offering on Mount Moriah (Gen. 22:2). Can you imagine Abraham's consternation? He must have wondered if he could possibly have heard God right! How would the promise ever be fulfilled if he obeyed? Yet there must have been no doubt as to the message because the Scriptures tell us he got up early in the morning, took his servants and his son and some wood for the burnt offering, and set off for Mount Moriah.

Abraham's obedience and faith astound me. But if Abraham's obedience, willing though agonized, is astounding, Isaac's willing subjection is even more amazing! Isaac was no toddler at the time of this event. He was probably a strong young teenager, well able to resist his old father. But he allowed himself to be bound and laid on top of the funeral pyre! We are given the idea that Isaac had a good idea what Abraham had in mind. He had already mentioned the fact that they had the wood and the fire, but no offering. In answer to his inquiry, Abraham replied, "God Himself will provide the lamb for the burnt offering, my son" (Gen. 22:8).

I'm sure Abraham was hoping a voice would stay his hand. But when no voice came, he continued with his incredible mission of plunging a knife through his precious son's heart. At the last moment, when God saw His servant was willing to surrender his most precious possession on earth, He stopped him. Abraham heard the voice of God, "Abraham! Abraham! . . . Do not lay a hand on the boy. . . . Do not do anything to him. Now I know that you fear God, because you have not withheld from Me your son, your only son" (Gen. 22:11-12). As Abraham looked about, he saw a ram caught by his horns in a thicket. God had provided a substitute. With unbelievable relief and joy, the two rejoined the servants and returned home. Abraham called that place "The LORD Will Provide"—or Jehovah-Jireh (Gen. 22:14).

This picture points to another day on the same Mount Moriah—the site of the temple sacrifices pointing down history to the cross of Calvary. This time it was God's Son—His only Son, that was placed upon His funeral pyre shaped like a cross. However, there was no voice from heaven at the last minute to stay the executioner's hand. God showed through this story of Abraham and Isaac what it would cost Him to take away our sin. He Himself provided the sacrifice—His Lamb.

I often think of the ram caught in the thicket. When I think about that animal, I am immediately reminded of how Jesus was willingly caught in the tangle of my sin, in order to be at the right place at the right time in history, to be my Jehovah-Jireh. God provided His Son so that His holiness and righteousness may be satisfied. He died so I could go free. Put yourself on that altar in your mind. That is what you deserve. Bound by sin, a just Judge pronounces the penalty— death. But look up—see the ram caught in the thicket—and thank Him!

Perhaps you don't know how to thank Him. Do you believe you have done anything worthy of the death penalty? Jehovah is so holy that only holiness like His can bring a reprieve from death. Sin is coming short of this holiness of life. As Jehovah banished Adam and Eve from the Garden of Eden, so He must banish us from heaven unless we pay the penalty for our sin. The penalty is a giving of life. Jesus, the Lamb of God that takes away the sin of the world, is the One the Father provided as our substitute. To say thank You is to personally acknowledge that His death was necessary to allow us to be forgiven. To say thank You to Jesus is to realize, as Isaac realized, that we can live because another has died! Thank Him with me now.

•TALKING IT OVER•

*Suggested
Times*

---

1. READ AND LIST.
   Read Genesis 28:10-20.
   ☐ List three things you learned from this passage
   about God's character.
   ☐ List three things you learned about Jacob's
   character.

10 minutes

---

2. REVIEW AND DISCUSS.
   Look up these verses and recap what they teach
   about the name Jehovah:
   ☐ Exodus 3:13-16
   ☐ Exodus 6:2-3
   ☐ Leviticus 19:2

5 minutes

---

3. REFLECT.
   Read Genesis 22:1-19. What do you learn about:
   ☐ Abraham?
   ☐ Isaac?
   ☐ Yourself?

10 minutes

---

4. PRAY.
   Using sentence prayers, talk conversationally with
   God. Start with praise; next pray for others, and
   then yourself.

5 minutes

•PRAYING IT THROUGH•

*Suggested
Times*

1. (As a group) Praise God for:
   - ☐ The particular characteristics of God's nature revealed by the name Jehovah.
   - ☐ The examples of Abraham and Isaac.
   - ☐ Christ, our Lamb, the substitute God provided for us.

5 minutes

2. (In twos) Pray for:
   - ☐ People who don't think the cross of Christ is necessary and are therefore left without a substitute for their sin.
   - ☐ People who are being tested with hard things, especially with their children.
   - ☐ People who believe in a transcendent God, but need to know Him in a personal way.

5 minutes

3. (In twos) Fill in the acrostic with ideas of how Jesus is Jehovah. For example: J–Jesus is our Saviour; E–Entered our world as a baby.
   J
   E
   H
   O
   V
   A
   H

5 minutes

4. (On your own) Meditate on:
   - ☐ Genesis 22:1-19
   - ☐ Luke 23:32-43

5 minutes

•DIGGING DEEPER•

Jehovah-Jireh (Gen. 22:1-19)

1. Read Exodus 3:1-15. Put yourself in Moses' shoes. What would he need to know about God to fulfill God's demand that he have the courage to face Pharaoh and the Israelites?

What must this particular name of God in Exodus 3:14 have communicated to Moses, enabling him to face his greatest fear and do what he absolutely did not want to do?

From this passage we learn God wants His people to know Him as the God who will be here for them and who will be with them. What encouragement does this give you today?

Why do you think Moses needed to be assured of God's presence to complete the task to which He was calling him?

Recall a difficult task God has required of you. How could knowing that God indeed is Jehovah have helped you accomplish His calling?

2. Read Genesis 22:1-19. In what ways was God's request in verses 1 and 2 contrary to His character and revelation?

List all the proofs of Abraham's faith in these 19 verses. Then state how Abraham illustrates the principle found in James 2:14-24.

What did Abraham learn about God through this immense test of his faith?

According to verse 14 what did Abraham choose to name the place of his greatest personal crisis? What does this name reveal about God's character?

Did Abraham understand God to be a personal God? Explain your answer using Scripture to support it.

3. What has been the greatest test of your faith so far in your Christian life? How did God provide for you? Go back and name the mountain of your crisis, a name which reflects what you learned about God there.

4. Abraham believed God would provide despite evidence to the contrary. What is God asking you to believe Him for? In prayer ask God to help you take your focus off the obstacles and to keep it on His countless provisions in your life.

For Further Study
1. Read the notes for Exodus 3:14-15 in a study Bible, preferably the *New International Version*. Find out what New Testament figure quoted these same words (3:14). Discover what word is incorrectly spelled **Jehovah.**
2. Ask God to show you what it is that you may be withholding from Him. Seek His strength to relinquish your Isaac.

•TOOL CHEST•
(A Suggested Optional Resource)

STUDY BIBLE

Once you have a study Bible you will wonder how you ever got along without it. Maps, concordance, cross-references, indexes, tables, and chronological charts are merely a few of the numerous helps available to you in this tool. Ask your pastor or Christian bookstore dealer to explain to you the theological bent of the study Bibles available. They will vary depending on the persuasion of their contributors and publishers. A word of caution is to keep in mind that the notes, however helpful, are not inspired. Only the biblical text itself is God's authoritative Word. Shop around before making this major investment, but do not delay. A study Bible will richly enhance your study of the Scriptures. A few study Bibles to consider are:

> *New American Standard Bible* (Holman)
> *The New English Bible* (Oxford University Press)
> *The NIV Study Bible* (Zondervan)
> *Ryrie Study Bible* (Moody)
> *Thompson Chain Reference Bible–King James Version* (B.B. Kirkbride Co., Inc.)

4
Jehovah-Rophe

•FOOD FOR THOUGHT•

Once they passed through the Red Sea, the Children of Israel surely expected to see the Promised Land. Instead they were treated to a very unfriendly landscape indeed. Their redemption had been incredible. Jehovah-Jireh had been all that was needed as the occasion had arisen. The lamb had been slain and the blood applied to the posts of the door of the Israelites' homes. Then the Angel of Death had passed over them, striking only those homes that were not covered by the blood.

Redemption had meant that the promise of God to Moses had been fulfilled. God had parted the Red Sea, and the Israelites had gone over on dry land, while the pursuing Egyptians were cast into the depths of the sea. And now the people were on the other side of redemption! The joy was intense. Great songs of praise and triumph rent the air. Miriam led the choir singing, "Sing to the LORD, for He is highly exalted. The horse and its rider He has hurled into the sea" (Ex. 15:21).

On that first day, the people stepped out into the Desert of Shur with great excitement. The second day, a different reaction set in, and on the third day, joy had fled and the situation became desperate. It didn't take the people long to begin grumbling about being on the other side of redemption.

Can we identify with these people? Do we remember what it was like to find Christ? To gain an understanding of the cross and the realization that the Lamb had been slain for our sins? Once we found faith in Christ we expected the Garden of Eden to be waiting for us on the other side of redemption! So what happened? Did we find ourselves in a desert instead of a garden, developing a terrible thirst that nothing would quench? Then did we see a small oasis on the horizon—Marah—a place of provision in our desert of delusion?

Did the Christians we looked to disappoint us, or the church we joined let us down? Did life suddenly deal us a cruel, sharp blow that sent us reeling down in the dust? Did we become bitter and resentful toward God and our church leaders, grumbling and complaining about it all? Did we feel desperately disappointed in God? If we answer yes to these questions, we need to remember that most of us who know the Lord have camped at Marah—on the other side of redemption!

A young girl complained to me that her life was fine until she accepted the Lord. Then the sky fell in. Her fiancé dumped her, her father died, and her best friend moved to the other side of the country! She was not expecting such treatment from God, from her fiancé, or from her friend.

"It was better in Egypt," she said bitterly. It is very interesting to me that it is at this point in history (just past the Red Sea) that Jehovah revealed Himself to Israel, as **Jehovah-Rophe,** "the God that heals." It is striking because it was not physical healing that was necessary! Wouldn't you have thought that the first time God leans out of heaven to tell mankind He is the Great Physician, it would be in connection with our bodies? But it wasn't! It was at the point of Israel's dashed dreams, hampered hopes, and desperate desires that He came and healed their bitter, disappointed, critical spirits.

This passage seems to indicate that the most important sickness God has to deal with is a spiritual malady. It is our sin nature that causes us to turn against God at the slightest cause. Sin is at the root of all mankind's maladies—physical, social, spiritual, and psychological.

God Himself is eternally healthy in every dimension of His being and is the source and provider of all health for His universe and those of us who live in it. It is sin that is the root cause of the dying bodies we all inherit, but redemption rolls back the curse of the fall. Can we ever doubt that God is the Great Physician when we see Jesus touching lepers, opening the eyes of the blind, and making lame men walk? But bodies last a lifetime, souls live forever, and the Great Physician is intent on bringing life to lost souls and renewing the bitter spirits of His saints.

Because we have unrealistic expectations, we are often unprepared when trouble comes. The Israelites camped just beyond the Red Sea, stopping with one foot almost in the water and one foot on sand! It was a suitable temporary campsite, but they were not supposed to stay there. If they were to reach Canaan, they had to camp at Marah on the way there!

Someone has determined that Moses was in charge of approximately 2 million souls, as well as cattle and baggage. It was only about 33 miles from the banks of the Red Sea to Marah, but the vast company of people had to move at a very slow pace, taking three days for this particular part of the journey. That would be like moving the entire population of Milwaukee and its suburbs 33 miles north, halfway to the Wisconsin state capital of Madison!

So Marah was definitely on the map as far as God was concerned. It was part of His plan. The people would undoubtedly have taken as much water as possible with them, but on the third day it was all gone. It is no wonder that the Israelites became bitter when they discovered that the water was bitter.

Yet God would not let the people bypass Marah. Having arrived at the polluted springs, the people were dismayed and angry! Now what were they going to do? God showed Moses a branch which he cast into the brackish water, sweetening it suddenly and miraculously.

God wanted to teach the Israelites a salutary lesson. He is Jehovah-rophe and He can certainly keep us in good health and make us whole if we are sick. But another dimension of wholeness is the miraculous ability to stay healthy in spirit when we are sick in body, and God used this opportunity to teach His people about that!

When God allows us to lack the essentials of healthy living, it is for His own secret reasons. We need to know one or two things that will really help us at those times. First of all, it is God's wish that we are always healthy. If the Apostle John could express that sentiment in his third letter, saying, "Dear friend, I pray that you may enjoy good health and that all may go well with you, even as your soul is getting along well" (3 John 2), then certainly Jehovah would wish it!

The Old Testament, however, presents two basic views concerning healing and sickness. First, the Old Testament considers Jehovah alone the source of health and sickness. The teaching of the Mosaic covenant said that sickness is the result of the entrance of sin into the world. Because of sin, man continues to rebel, the result of which may be punishment by sickness (Deut. 28:22, 58-61; 32:39). Obedience, on the other hand, will be rewarded by good health (Ex. 23:22-25). The second view presented in the Old Testament is that suffering is a consequence of the corrupt nature of man because of original sin (Gen. 2:17; 3:19). In other words, when Adam sinned, man became naturally susceptible to disease.

Jesus based His teaching about healing on the second viewpoint without negating the teaching contained in the Mosaic covenant. He said that sickness is not *always* punishment for sin, though it is a possible result (John 5:14). When Jesus saw a blind man sitting by the side of the road one day and His disciples asked Him if the man's blindness was a result of his sin, Jesus replied that it wasn't (John 9:1-3). The New Testament illustrates how God works through sickness to discipline and chasten His children and to produce in them the fruits of the Spirit (2 Cor. 4:17). Nevertheless, suffering is basically an evil that thoroughly contradicts and hinders God's best wishes and will for mankind.

We cannot doubt God loves to be our Jehovah-Rophe, but we need to remember that everyone healed in the Old Testament as well as those who were healed by Jesus in the New Testament died. Their bodies only lasted a lifetime, but their souls live forever.

The name Elohim tells us that the Trinity promised each other that whatever was broken would be mended. Romans 8:18-37 and Revelation 7:15-17 speak of the final day when everything will be healed in heaven and in earth. Till then we may experience healing *in measure* on the way to healing *forever*. It will be in heaven then that there will be *no more* sickness, whereas here on earth there will certainly be *some 'more* until we're through!

After the bittersweet experience at Marah, the Children of Israel journeyed on toward Elim, a fragrant, flourishing oasis. What a contrast they found there! Two beautiful springs and 70 palm trees were waiting to refresh them. It wasn't very far from Marah either. But then, blessing is never very far from bitterness!

Where are you living at the moment? At Marah or Elim? If you are living at Marah, try to travel on a bit in your Christian walk till you reach Elim! Let Jehovah-Rophe deal with the waters of bitterness that have made you sick, sweetening them with His cross, reminding you that He died to provide you with all that you need as the occasion arises!

If you are living at Elim, remember Marah and don't grow complacent. Canaan is ahead and there is a lot of desert in between! Perhaps you are thinking of settling down at Elim and forgetting all about moving on! Ah, but God never allows us to settle down anywhere in this life. We are strangers and pilgrims and there is much land yet to be possessed. Drink deeply at Elim and rest awhile. Then pick up your spiritual suitcases and head out for the Promised Land. Whatever happens to you on the way, you can be sure Jehovah-Rophe will be there!

•TALKING IT OVER•

Suggested Times

---

1. READ AND REVIEW.   *5 minutes*
   Read Exodus 15:1-5. Discuss "the other side of
   redemption."
   ☐ What has your experience been like since
      you've been a believer?
   ☐ Did you find disappointments awaiting you?

---

2. DISCUSS.   *10 minutes*
   Read the story in Exodus 16:2-36. What does this
   teach you about:
   ☐ The Lord's attitude?
   ☐ The people's attitude?
   ☐ Moses' and Aaron's attitudes?
   ☐ Your attitude?

---

3. SHARE.   *3 minutes*
   Recall:
   ☐ One thing you want to remember about Jeho-
      vah-Rophe.
   ☐ One thing you would like to tell others about
      Him and why.

---

4. LIST.   *7 minutes*
   Make a list of sick people. Pray for one of them.
   Then make a list of well people who need to stay
   well and pray for one of them.

---

5. ON YOUR OWN.   *5 minutes*
   Write a little note to God about a bad attitude you
   have had about something or someone. Ask Him
   to forgive you.

• PRAYING IT THROUGH •

*Suggested
Times*

1. (On your own) Praise the Lord for:
   □ Your Passover Lamb
   □ Your redemption
   □ Satan's defeat

   2 minutes

2. (In twos) Pray for Christians living at Marah, who have bitter, complaining attitudes. Pray about your own attitude.

   2 minutes

3. (As a group) Keeping in mind that God is Jehovah-Rophe, pray for people who are:
   □ Physically sick
   □ Emotionally sick
   □ Spiritually sick

   4 minutes

4. (On your own) Read Revelation 7:15-17 and contemplate the final healing.

   4 minutes

5. (In twos) Share with a partner the need someone you know has to read these verses. Pray about it together.

   4 minutes

6. (On your own) Make a prayer list for the week. List three things or people for each day.
   Monday
   Tuesday
   Wednesday
   Thursday
   Friday
   Saturday
   Sunday

   4 minutes

•DIGGING DEEPER•

Jehovah-Rophe (Ex. 15:22-27)

1. Read Exodus 15:22-27. What is the context of this incident?

How many miracles had God performed through His servant Moses to attain Pharaoh's attention?

What would the Israelites have learned about God when they were preserved from the plagues?

2. Read Exodus 14:21 and imagine the story as if it were a movie. Picture the wall of water, like a tidal wave, on either side of the people as they crossed the seabed. Determine the width of the dry land it would have required to allow 2 million people (plus animals and belongings) to cross the Red Sea during the night. How would the sobering scene in verse 30 have affected you?

Describe the emotions Moses and Miriam were experiencing when they broke into song. If your ancestors had been in captivity for 400 years and you were suddenly free, what song might you compose?

3. There is certainly an element of surprise in verses 22-24. What is so shocking?

Why would God intentionally lead them to Marah?

How would you have expected the Israelites to have responded to this adversity?

4. Just three days after witnessing the greatest feat of their lifetime, the Israelites were quick to grumble and complain. How would you describe the character of these people?

What was their sin?

What had they forgotten about God? How could they so easily forget?

Are you quick to forget God's provisions in your own life? What have you complained about this week?

5. How would you expect God to respond to the Israelites' poor attitude and lack of trust in Him?

List the attributes of God you observe in this passage.

6. What truth would the miracle at Marah have communicated to this doubting people?

How was this crisis a test? (v. 25) Support your answer with Scripture.

Is God testing you? If so, why, and what is He teaching you by it?

7. How did God show Himself to be true to His name, Jehovah-Rophe? From what had He kept the Israelites? From what would He keep them? Was His promise conditional?

8. Describe the contrast between Marah and Elim. Why did God lead the Israelites from barren desert to lush paradise?

   Has God brought you to Elim by way of Marah? What is Jehovah-Rophe teaching you through these experiences?

9. Do you need to take an attitude check? Do you need to know God as Jehovah-Rophe? Spend a few moments in prayer about these matters and then reflect on Psalm 23.

For Further Study
1. Become a student of the wilderness wanderings. Study the biblical stories of those 40 years and the lessons learned. Make your own map of the geography visited.
2. Examine the notes on Exodus 15:25 in a study Bible. Define the "law" and the "decree" mentioned in this verse.
3. Read an Old Testament history/survey on the period of Israel's desert wanderings.

•TOOL CHEST•
(A Suggested Optional Resource)

SURVEYS AND HISTORIES

A Survey of Israel's History (Zondervan) by Dr. Leon J. Wood and David J. O'Brien introduces the reader to Old Testament background, themes, and relevant archaeological information in layman's terms. Chapter 7 specifically covers the period of Israel's desert wanderings. If you have ever been curious as to what Israel did to turn a 150-mile journey into a 40-year trek, Wood's survey will help you solve the mystery. Maps are provided to trace the journey, and details on Marah and Elim are included. You will want to acquaint yourself with the many insights on the Law and tabernacle found in this pertinent text. Other histories and Old Testament surveys you may wish to compare include:

A *History of Israel* by John Bright (Westminster)
Israel and the Nations by F.F. Bruce (Eerdmans)
An Historical Survey of the Old Testament by Eugene H. Merrill (Baker)
Old Testament History by Charles F. Pfeiffer (Zondervan)
Willmington's Survey of the Old Testament by H.L. Willmington (Victor)

5
Jehovah-Nissi

•FOOD FOR THOUGHT•

A difficult experience at Rephidim gave Jehovah one more opportunity to let the Israelites get to know Him a little bit better during their long trek. Once more the water jars were empty. The sun had not stopped beating down on the Israelites' heads, and drought led to doubt. On arriving at Rephidim, the people found the wells dry! At Marah there had been bitter water; here there was no water at all. It seems that the Israelites would have learned their lesson by now. God had come through wonderfully so far. In fact, He had been marvelously active in their very recent past—why should He fail them now? But every time the people went around a corner, they grumbled and turned against Moses all over again. "They are almost ready to stone me," Moses complained to the Lord (Ex. 17:4). We should always be careful about our grumbling because, like measles, it's catching! Even Moses was affected by the constant griping around him.

The way God's people went from drought to doubt to delight to drought and doubt again should come as no surprise to those of us who, if honest, have the same unstable spiritual experience. Some of us find ourselves wandering round and round in the wilderness of inconsistency, just as the Israelites did. The crises that God allows to come into our lives help us to get to know Him, as well as ourselves, better.

What a blessing God doesn't change every time He goes around a corner! Remember Jehovah's name means the Unchanging One; He is who He is now and forever. What is more, because He is the Rock smitten for us to supply us with the water of life, He can help us to be consistent too. Paul probably was thinking of this incident when he said, "They all ate the same spiritual food and drank the same spiritual drink; for they drank from the spiritual rock that accompanied them, and that rock was Christ" (1 Cor. 10:3-4).

So Israel needn't have grumbled so much. God was working it all out. He was standing on the rock in Rephidim waiting for them to arrive. He was proving Himself to be all that was needed as the occasion arose! But no sooner had the amazed Israelites quenched their parched throats, than a cry of fear went up from the outskirts of the camp. Amalek had arrived. It was not their week!

Who were these mean and powerful people called Amalekites? In Genesis 36:12, we discover that Amalek was the grandson of Esau and therefore a direct descendent of Isaac. The Amalekites had been one of the first nations to oppose Israel and had always been a problem to the people of God (Num. 24:20). Their methods were less than gentlemanly: "Remember what the Amalekites did to you along the way when you came out of Egypt. When you were weary and worn out, they met you on your journey and cut off all who were lagging behind; they had no fear of God" (Deut. 25:17-18). They used guerrilla tactics as well as open warfare. They would sneak up behind the huge group of people and pick off the weakest.

God declared Himself against Amalek and his descendants from generation to generation. "Then the LORD said to Moses, 'Write this on a scroll as something to be remembered and make sure that Joshua hears it, because I will completely blot out the memory of Amalek from under heaven.' Moses built an altar and called it The LORD is my Banner. He said, 'For hands were lifted up to the throne of the LORD. The LORD will be at war against the Amalekites from generation to generation' " (Ex. 17:14-16). God, knowing the future as well as the past, knew that if the Amalekites were not destroyed, they would seek to do away with God's people whenever they could.

Saul had been told to exterminate the Amalekites, but he disobeyed God's orders. It gives us food for thought to realize that one of the people Saul spared returned to kill him (2 Sam. 1:1-16). Then there was Haman, a descendent of the Amalekites. He tried, like some ancient Hitler, to destroy every Jew in sight in Esther's day.

At Rephidim, God told Israel to go and fight the Amalekites. The Israelites belonged to Jehovah. This was His cause and His battle. He had, after all, declared war on Amalek from generation to generation.

Israel did well—at last! Under Joshua's capable leading, the best of Israel's men set out to fight their ancient enemy. Moses, vindicated by producing water from the rock, discovered that the people were happy for once to follow his orders. So he climbed a hill with the rod of God in his hand, while Joshua fought Amalek in the valley below him.

Moses held the rod high in the sky so that the men glancing up could see it gleaming in the sunlight. This rod was a symbol and pledge of Jehovah's presence and power. This was the rod used to bring plagues on Pharaoh and part the Red Sea, allowing the Children of Israel to go through on dry ground. Seeing Moses on the hillside stretching that rod out over the valley would have been an incentive to any soldier fighting for his life below.

But Moses' arms became as heavy as lead, so Aaron and Hur came alongside and supported his arms. In this way, the battle was won. For when Moses let the rod fall, Israel did poorly, but when he raised the rod high, Israel raised themselves up against their enemies.

What is the application of all of this? Jehovah revealed Himself to Israel at Rephidim as **Jehovah-Nissi, the LORD my Banner.** How can such information make a difference in our mundane lives? The whole story gives us a picture of our own spiritual warfare. Remember Esau was the man who despised spiritual things. Therefore, Amalek represents our worldly nature as well as the forces against the King and His kingdom here on earth. Within us all lurks an enemy like Amalek. Paul calls that enemy our "old man" or "old nature." It is the self that is at war with the Spirit of God. The spirit of Satan joins forces with the spirit of Amalek, or the flesh within us, and tries to bury us.

Jehovah, however, lifts up a banner against Amalek and rallies believers to His cause. Israel is a picture of you and of me. Those of us who love the Lord need to know there is a fight to be fought. We have our part to play even as Joshua and Israel's soldiers had their part to play. Once we are on the other side of redemption, we have work to do. We need to put on the armor of the Spirit in order to march against the worldly forces that would destroy us (Eph. 6:10-20). As Paul told Timothy, we are to "fight the good fight of the faith" (1 Tim. 6:12).

But how do we fight Amalek? We know we need to wear the "breastplate of righteousness" and take "the shield of faith" with which we can quench the fiery darts of the evil one (Eph. 6:14-16). But how shall we recognize the enemy when he comes?

We will recognize him in the same way that Israel recognized him. The leaders of Israel came to realize that Amalek used open warfare as well as guerrilla tactics. We won't have much doubt about who is attacking us if our boss makes a pass at us at work, if we are tempted to cheat at exams, or we are asked to tell a lie. That is open warfare!

Guerrilla tactics are much harder to cope with. Guerrillas ambush or snipe from the most unexpected places! Jesus tells us to "watch and pray" so that we will not fall into temptation (Matt. 26:41). Fighting a guerrilla war means being on our toes listening, looking about us, and watching our steps.

Amalek attacked Israel when they were weak. He hasn't changed his strategy today. There is a part of us that wants to be weak. The flesh cannot be reformed or trained to be a Christian. It is condemned already and deserves to die. We must put to death the misdeeds of the body or like Saul, the flesh may return to destroy us.

One way we can do this is to starve our enemy to death! The cuckoo is a bird that lays its eggs in another bird's nest. The unsuspecting "surrogate" hatches all the eggs and then tries to feed all the hungry chicks. The cuckoo is large and greedy so he usually grows stronger and stronger until he is able to push the natural birds out of the nest. It all depends on which bird the mother feeds!

So it is with us. If we would see Amalek defeated, we need to starve the fleshly nature to death. There will be books, plays, TV soaps, and perhaps even some "mind movies" (if we're too pious to go to the real ones) that we will need to starve out of our lives! Then we must work hard at feeding the new nature we have received if we have been born from above.

Jehovah promises to raise His banner over us. This is His cause. He has declared war against Amalek from generation to generation. He is not content to see Amalek picking us off when we lag behind the crowd or are spiritually weak. He would encourage us to remember the rod of God, His power, and His people. We need our support group just as Moses and Joshua needed Aaron and Hur holding up their holy hands in prayer. None of us can do without that sort of support when we are dealing with Amalek.

Most of all, we will need to understand God is for us. He is Jehovah-Nissi, the One who will be all that we need as the occasion arises. When we are attacked by an overwhelming fleshly desire, we must remember and obey what His servant Moses said, "Go out to fight the Amalekites" (Ex. 17:9).

•TALKING IT OVER•

*Suggested
Times*

1. READ AND LIST.
Read Exodus 17:1-16.
☐ List all the reasons the Children of Israel had to trust God. Why do you think they still grumbled?
☐ List all the reasons you have to trust God. What then should be your attitude?

6 minutes

2. REVIEW.
Review all you know about Amalek.
☐ Read Deuteronomy 25:17-18 and compare this situation with the way the "flesh" attacks us.
☐ Review Exodus 17:14-16. What is the most important thought from these verses?

6 minutes

3. READ AND SHARE.
☐ Read Romans 7:14-25. What is Paul talking about? Share an example of this principle from your own life.
☐ Read Romans 8:5-14. Share your favorite verse from this passage.

10 minutes

4. PRACTICE.
☐ Get in twos and pretend your partner is a non-believer who is succumbing to temptation. Without using Scripture phrases, tell her what you think God wants her to know.
☐ Pretend your partner is a believer who is struggling with the flesh. Use your Bible to show her a verse and urge her to stand firm.
Pray together.

8 minutes

•PRAYING IT THROUGH•   *Suggested Times*

1. (As a group) Praise God for: *3 minutes*
   □ Victory in the Christian life.
   □ A promise verse from Romans 8:5-14.

2. (As a group) Pray for believers attacked by Ama-   *3 minutes*
   lek or desires of the flesh.

3. (In twos) Share a weakness you need God's power   *4 minutes*
   to overcome. Pray about it.

4. (On your own) Make a list of fleshly temptations   *4 minutes*
   that face the following people today:
   □ Young people
   □ Elderly people
   □ Married couples
   □ Children
   Pray for people you know who are in these cate-
   gories.

5. (On your own) Pray silently, praising God that He   *6 minutes*
   is Jehovah-Nissi.

• DIGGING DEEPER •

Jehovah-Nissi (Ex. 17:1-16)

1. Read Exodus 17:1-7. What unmet needs did the Israelites have? How did they go about getting their needs met?

Describe the unhealthy pattern the nation was developing for having their needs met.

What was wrong with this method?

Describe the correct way to ask God to meet our needs (Phil. 4:6-7).

2. How do you usually handle unmet needs and unfulfilled desires?

Which areas of your life are you most prone to complain about? (finances, health, job, ministry, family, etc.)

To whom do you usually complain?

What is keeping you from going directly to God and presenting your complaint in the manner recommended in Philippians 4:6-7?

3. According to Moses, the people guilty of what? (Ex. 17:2)

What can we learn about being quarrelsome from these references?

4. In what way did the Israelites put God to the test? Why was this wrong?

Do you ever test God? If so, how?

5. Israel's need was very great, a matter of life and death. Did the need justify the means? Why or why not? (Ps. 95:8-11; Heb. 3:7-11, 16-19)

Are you trying to meet a need by unjust means? Do you often find yourself justifying your methods of meeting needs?

In a written prayer, admit your fault and agree with God that it is sin. Ask His help to employ only appropriate means and to eliminate the desire to justify and defend yourself to others.

6. Evaluate Moses' response to the Israelites' grumbling (Ex. 17:4). What provoked such exasperation? What did Moses do with his concern that the Israelites should have done?

7. How did the Israelites misunderstand God's nature? (Ex. 17:3)

What was the real heart of the problem with the Israelites? (Ex. 17:7)

When God has to lead you in a specific direction, are you tempted to doubt His leading, presence, or goodness?

8. What did the miracle in Exodus 17:6 prove to this "wishy-washy" nation?

What evidence does God often give you to confirm His leading?

9. Read Exodus 17:8-15. What do you think was the major lesson to be learned from this event?

What did the staff symbolize?

How did the Israelites win the battle?

10. Have you had a Rephidim experience lately where you have had to completely depend on the presence and Banner of the Lord? If not, take a risk and ask God to be your Banner in a significant battle you are facing.

For Further Study
Memorize the names of God and corresponding Bible references and themes of each reference which you have studied so far.

•TOOL CHEST•
(A Suggested Optional Resource)

THE ENIGMA OF EVIL
Have you ever struggled answering tough questions such as: Why do bad things happen to good people? Why do the ungodly flourish? How can God be good when there is so much suffering in the world? Does God really care for me? If you struggle with questions such as these, perhaps you should give John W. Wenham's *The Enigma of Evil* (Zondervan) your consideration. Thought-provoking in content, this tool wades with integrity through the floodwaters of life and will guide you to higher ground. Bring your Rephidim questions to the reading of this book. It will truly help you to genuinely acknowledge that God is indeed your Banner.

6
Jehovah-Shalom

•FOOD FOR THOUGHT•

In His own person, Jehovah is perfect peace. Even though He is grieved at sin, moved to wrath at evil, and touched with the feelings of our infirmities, nothing can unsteady the perfect balance of His divine nature. In his book *Names of God* (Moody), Nathan Stone says God "could never give to others a peace that passes understanding if He was not perfect unfailing peace Himself." Because Jehovah loves us and wants to bless us, He wants us to know this extraordinary peace that He Himself enjoys.

So what exactly is this peace we are talking about? What precisely does the Hebrew word *shalom* imply? My husband Stuart says that peace is not necessarily the absence of conflict, but is rather **the tranquility of order.** This implies the idea of getting it all together, of healthy, complete composure. Many times shalom is translated "perfect" and speaks of wholeness or harmony with God. It is used, of course, in the phrase **peace offering,** and that offering speaks of a blood sacrifice, or a life shed prior to a time when God and man can be reconciled once again. A restoration of fellowship is indicated; a peace lost by the Fall, restored through Jehovah-Jireh, providing for Himself a Lamb.

The search for peace expresses the deepest desire and need of the human heart. It is the great name of the Messiah. When our God reigns, His presence brings peace to our troubled lives. Jerusalem is the city of the Messiah, and the familiar name means city of peace. So shalom, the most common form of greeting in Bible lands to this day, carries with it the wish for peace of mind and heart and life for the one being greeted. Jehovah's presence is indeed a peaceful thing, and we could not wish anything better for those we meet along life's way.

Jehovah *is* Peace. He also brings peace. After Joshua's death, the land of Canaan was divided and conquered. But little national peace or unity existed. There was no central government and no centralized worship. In fact, the Bible, summing up the prevailing attitude of the day, reports, "everyone did as he saw fit" (Jud. 17:6).

The people took no notice of God and intermarried, mingling their precious faith with the heathen religions of the people living around them. Jehovah had already appeared to their ancestors as Jehovah-Meqaddish, meaning "the Lord that sanctifies." The word **sanctify,** meaning "set apart," brought a message that Israel didn't care to heed. So the Lord gave them into the hands of heathen kings until they cried out in grief. They were then rescued by Jehovah, who raised up a series of judges to lead them to independence again. Othniel, Ehud, Shamgar, Deborah, and Gideon were some of these leaders. God had pity on His people and visited them with deliverance.

When we reach Judges 6, we find that the Midianites were giving Israel a really hard time. They burned the people's crops, stole their cattle, and plundered their tents, until the people took refuge in the caves of the mountains and the holes in the ground. One day Gideon was winnowing barley in a wine press. Apparently he didn't do it openly, because the enemy would have seen him and soon arrived to destroy him as well as his crops.

The Angel of the LORD (a manifestation of Jehovah Himself in human form) appeared to Gideon and greeted him with the words, "The LORD is with you, mighty warrior" (Jud. 6:12). I'm sure the Angel of the LORD had a wry smile on His face as He greeted Gideon in this way. Gideon probably did not *feel* like a mighty warrior. In fact, he resisted saying, "My clan is the weakest in Manasseh, and I am the least in my family" (Jud. 6:15). The truth of the matter was that Gideon really was a mighty man of valor—he just didn't know it yet! At that particular moment in time, Gideon was fearful with lots of questions about the sad state of the economy, national affairs, and his own well-being. "If You really have been with us all along as You say," he seemed to ask, "then *why* have all these bad things happened to us?" Quite a normal question under the circumstances, don't you think?

I know a lot of people who have Gideon questions these days— people who have had a tough deal in life; parents whose children have left home and never contacted them again; wives whose husbands have walked out on them and refused to pay child support; men who have been cheated on by their wives; teenage victims of date rape. For those people to believe that God was with them in their past and is with them now is a really tough assignment. Like Gideon, they are tempted to ask, "Why has all this happened to us?"

Of course, God listened carefully to Gideon's response to His greeting and answered him. Observing that the hard things in Gideon's life had resulted in a lack of faith, the Lord merely said, "Go in the strength you have" (Jud. 6:14). God is content to take us where we are and work with us. Gideon had only a little faith, but God assured him it was enough for His purposes, and began to strengthen him for the job that lay ahead.

It is worthy to note that God can never bring peace through us until He has brought peace to us. When the Lord Jesus stilled the storm, Mark's Gospel tells us that "there were also other boats with Him" (Mark 4:36). All the boats experienced the storm, including the one with Jesus on board. As soon as Jesus stilled the storm, however, we can assume that peace came to all the other boats as well. To be the source of peace for others in conflict will depend much on the personal peace that has been experienced in our own lives.

Jehovah brings peace to the man or woman who builds an altar in his or her heart and says, "I'll go to war on behalf of the Lord, and Jehovah will be my peace." Gideon went to war and discovered he was indeed a mighty warrior and just didn't know it!

It is a funny thing but as soon as we give in and do what God wants us to do, we often walk straight into conflict. How can the Prince of Peace bring conflict? Well, that is exactly what Jesus said would happen as soon as we went out into our world to fight the good fight of faith!

Often this conflict arises in our families. It is especially difficult when our obedience to the Lord results in conflict in the family. When Gideon was told to break down his father's altars and sacrifice his father's bull to Jehovah, no one could really blame him for waiting till the dark hours of the night to comply. But Gideon realized that "peace at any price" would not bring eternal peace to the souls of these he loved, and we have to realize that truth as well.

I have had a dear family member say to me, "Jill, I feel a thousand miles away from you." I knew exactly what this person meant. When we have to cut down our dear ones' sacred beliefs because we know the truth and perceive the error in their religious philosophy, that's a potentially divisive thing to do! And yet, even in the midst of family conflict, we can build an altar in our hearts and know the shalom of Jehovah. If we really love those people, we will find the strength to break down their altars, burn their Asherah poles, and suffer the consequences those actions may bring.

It is interesting to note that Gideon's father was not as angry as Gideon obviously expected him to be! As it turned out, the son's obedience brought at last national peace to his country, which of course his father benefited from.

Because the things God was asking Gideon to do were difficult things, he wanted to make sure he was getting God's instructions right, and the Lord was more than willing to confirm His directions. We do not have to shear a sheep and lay its wool on the ground to see if it's wet in the morning. We are blessed with Bibles to read and other Christians to advise us as well as many helpful aids to help us discern God's will in our lives. Ways that Gideon probably never dreamed about! Suffice it to say, when we are ready to go to war to bring peace to our world, God will give us the tools and a team to finish the job.

Gideon started off with thousands to help him fight the hoards of Midianites. He ended up with a handful of dedicated soldiers. Together they routed Israel's enemies and won the day. They brought peace to their land, and Gideon became their leader and hero. Amazingly, they did it all with trumpets and jars containing lighted lamps. When Gideon gave the order, they blew the trumpets and broke the jars, and the light shone out into the darkness, bringing panic to the sleeping Midianites.

So shall it be with us. When we lift up our voices like trumpets and allow God to break us in order for His light to be released, we'll see and enjoy a great and glorious victory. So first, we must know the peace of God for ourselves, and then we must be obedient to His law and live broken and contrite lives before Him. Then and only then will Jehovah-Shalom rightly get the glory and become the God of those we love.

•TALKING IT OVER•

1. DISCUSS.   *5 minutes*
   ☐ Why do you think God chose Gideon?
   ☐ How does this encourage you?
   ☐ Why didn't God get fed up with the Israelites?

---

2. READ AND DISCUSS.   *10 minutes*
   Skim Judges 3–5.
   ☐ Which Judge did you like and why?
   ☐ Which didn't you like?

---

3. TALK.   *8 minutes*
   Read Judges 7 and discuss Gideon's experience
   with his soldiers.
   ☐ What do you think Gideon was thinking?
   ☐ What was God thinking?
   ☐ What were the men thinking?
   ☐ What are you thinking?

---

4. DISCUSS IN TWOS.   *3 minutes*
   Think about the ways God guides us.
   ☐ Review the "helps" God gives us.
   ☐ Talk about the "fleece" idea.

---

5. SHARE.   *4 minutes*
   Check the words below that express ways in
   which God has guided you.
   ☐ The Word of God
   ☐ Prayer
   ☐ Circumstances
   ☐ Advice of other Christians
   ☐ Common sense
   ☐ Inner conviction
   If appropriate, share something you need guid-
   ance about.

•PRAYING IT THROUGH•

Suggested Times

---

1. (On your own) Praise God for His peace-nature and what this means for:
   □ The world.
   □ Your family.
   □ You.
   Praise Him for:
   □ The peace He promises in conflicts.
   □ The opportunities and the situations He gives you to grow in grace.
   □ Being interested in your conflicts.

5 minutes

---

2. (As a group) Pray for people who are afraid:
   □ To make a stand with their families.
   □ To verbalize their faith.

5 minutes

---

3. (In twos) Share with one other person a conflict in your family. Then pray:
   □ That you will be able to hear God's voice guiding you.
   □ For a resolution to the conflict.
   □ For a chance to glorify the Lord because of the conflict.
   □ For endurance.
   □ For courage like Gideon's to do the right thing so your family will be blessed.

10 minutes

•DIGGING DEEPER•

Jehovah-Shalom (Jud. 6:1-24)

1. Read Judges 6:1-40. Then write a news release as if you were a reporter covering the events of 6:1-6.

2. What reason is given for the catastrophe in Judges 6?

3. Look up these ancient peoples in a Bible dictionary and write a brief synopsis for each.

   MIDIANITES:

   AMALEKITES:

   AMORITES:

4. What well-known New Testament truth does this episode from the life of Gideon illustrate?

Name an Old Testament patriarch who similarly objected to obeying God's request.

How valid were Gideon's concerns for the task God was asking of him? (v. 15)

Do you excuse your own unwillingness to accept ministry responsibilities or lack of attempting anything new for God? If so, on what basis? Are weakness and sense of inadequacy valid grounds for saying no?

5. In session 5 we saw that the Israelites were guilty of putting God to the test. Do you believe Gideon was guilty of the same? Please support your answer with Scripture. Can you be definitive about your conclusions?

6. Of all the self-revelations God could have given to Gideon, why did He choose peace? (v. 23) Explain why it was apropos to Gideon's circumstance.

7. Was Gideon wise or foolish to act for God in the night?

In what way are you too much like Gideon? Spend time in honest prayer before the Lord concerning these issues.

8. What effect did Gideon's stand actually have on his family? Why do you suppose Joash went to bat for his son?

9. Read Judges 7:1-25 and 8:28. How did Gideon grow in might?

How did God bring about peace among Gideon's family, neighborhood, and nation?

10. What principles for Christian living can you draw from the life of Gideon?

Is there a situation in your own life which needs the presence and reassurance of Jehovah-Shalom? What is God asking of you that may appear to cause discord, but with His supernatural help could actually bring about peace?

For Further Study
1. Complete your reading of Gideon's story in Judges 8:1-35. What qualities do you admire in this mighty warrior? What mistakes did he make?
2. Do a word study on the word **peace** using a Bible concordance. Share your results with your pastor and ask for his input.

•TOOL CHEST•
(A Suggested Optional Resource)

EVERYONE IN THE BIBLE
William P. Barker's *Everyone in the Bible* (Revell) will familiarize you with the men, women, and children who fill and illustrate the pages of Scripture. Biographical sketches on every single name appearing in the Bible are provided for the reader in this convenient catalog. A brief overview of each person's life and contribution to biblical truths along with references is contained in this well written Bible help.

7

Jehovah-Ro'i

•FOOD FOR THOUGHT•

Jehovah-Ro'i, meaning "Jehovah my Shepherd," appears for the first time in Psalm 23, one of the most universally loved portions of Scripture. The meaning and use of Ro'i is "to feed or lead to pasture, as a shepherd with his flock." It contains the obvious idea of leadership and caring. The word is also used figuratively in the Scriptures to indicate the relationship between a Prince and his people. For example, we read, "In the past, while Saul was king over us, you were the one who led Israel on their military campaigns. And the LORD said to you, 'You will shepherd My people Israel, and you will become their ruler' " (2 Sam. 5:2).

The Children of Israel knew very well what it was like to be shepherded by men who misused their power. Ezekiel uses the figure of the indolent shepherd to chastise the leaders of Israel. In Ezekiel 34 we find the prophet complaining that the spiritual and national leaders of God's people had only taken care of themselves. They had taken advantage of their position to "fleece" the flock, growing fat off the proceeds of their ministry and position, while starving the very people they were supposed to be feeding.

The Lord Himself complained through His prophet that they had not strengthened the weak, healed the sick, or bound up the injured among the flock entrusted to their care. They had neglected to search for the strays or the lost, and had ruled harshly and even brutally. "So, they were scattered because there was no shepherd" (Ezek. 34:4-5). When there is no shepherd to care for the sheep, the strays are preyed upon, wander about alone, and are exposed to dangerous and destructive forces.

This passage illustrates the high ideal of kingship in the Old Testament. It also helps us see that Jehovah-Ro'i was the true "King Shepherd" of Israel, whom the "under king shepherds" of

Israel were supposed to emulate. No wonder Jehovah-Ro'i was upset with the way that His leaders were reneging on their high and holy calling.

In contrast, Psalm 23 gives us the model of the Good Shepherd and the way He cares for His flock. This Psalm, written by David (King Shepherd of Israel and the one who perhaps came closest to the ideal), first speaks of the love, leading, and light provided by Jehovah-Ro'i for those who follow Him. What does a sheep need from his shepherd? Why, surely, first and foremost, love. The knowledge that somebody cares. The shepherd who makes his flock lie down in green pastures is the shepherd sheep love to follow if they are looking for true satisfaction in life. Our Heavenly Shepherd provides spiritual food for us in the Bible and satisfaction of soul through the living waters of life that speak of the Holy Spirit's inner working inside us.

Second, the Good Shepherd leads His flock. There is a sense of purpose in the way He lights our way. The right path for our feet is obvious if one is living close to Jehovah-Ro'i. As we hear His voice and obey, we find light in the valleys and sunshine on the hills.

As a Christian, Jehovah-Ro'i has guided my decisions in life. When I have come to a crossroad and perhaps had to choose which of two good ways was the best, He has led me to find the right answers to my hard questions.

Not only does Jehovah-Ro'i love His sheep and lead His sheep, He also promises to land His sheep safely in the heavenly fold. We are indeed on our way to a heavenly destination where we will "dwell in the house of the Lord forever" (Ps. 23:6). What comfort to know He plans for us an experience in the very presence of God that defies description, boggles the mind, and produces a fast pulse rate in a little sheep's breast! Until that day, we can be busy following our Jehovah-Ro'i, learning to be "king shepherds" ourselves and caring for those entrusted to our care! These two pictures challenge me constantly!

The idea of following our Shepherd in such a way as to grow strong enough to become under shepherds ourselves leaves us with work to do for the rest of our lives! With all our hearts and souls we should want to shepherd others in a way in which Jehovah-Ro'i would approve!

Are we Ezekiel 34 shepherds, or do we belong in Psalm 23? Do we only take care of our own souls, running to Bible studies and taking advantage of the flock, or do we lead others to the green pastures He has lovingly led us to? Do we bind up the injured, seek the strays, and rule fairly, or could we care less about anyone else who's having a hard time in life?

This leads us to the New Testament and the revelation of the Lord Jesus Christ as Jehovah-Ro'i in person. He, in His own words, is the Good Shepherd, the Perfect One, who gave His life for the sheep (John 10:15). Jesus "came to seek and to save what was lost" (Luke 19:10). He told His audience on one occasion that the Good Shepherd cares for the 1 sheep out of the 100 that goes astray or ends up in a hole! The Shepherd who owns the sheep leaves the 99 found ones, and at tremendous cost to Himself, seeks until He finds the lost one.

Some of us spend all our lives with the 99. We are called perhaps to nurture the found—to disciple Christians. We are tempted to forget the "one" or to think that person is another's responsibility. It is "safe" to involve ourselves with fold fellowship, rather than risk the wild animals and the elements to look for the lost. Yet shepherds do not only care for the found. The true nature of a shepherd is to always care as much about the 1 as he cares for the 99!

In the course of the work that the Lord has given to me, I have cause to spend 99 percent of my time among the 99! I speak to Christians, write for Christians, disciple Christians, travel with Christians, and basically have no occasion to even talk to the one stray in the course of a whole month! The gifts that God has given me are basically nurturing gifts. So I struggle to keep a true shepherd's heart and remember that in the middle of all the "blessed bleats" around me, I need to listen for the cry of the lamb who has no one to care for his soul.

As I worked on this part of this book, I found myself sitting in a very small plane, intent on finishing this chapter. I was aware suddenly that my little commuter plane had filled up with a boisterous crowd, focusing their attention on their weekend away, drinks, and having a good time. The jokes were flying; raucous, a little off color, and bawdy remarks about wives left behind and women ahead that would lighten their lives and provide diversions needed. How easy it would have been to keep on writing! How hard it would be to put away my pen and engage my companion in conversation, hoping to discover if Jehovah-Ro'i had led me to this particular seat on this particular plane, on this particular day, for this particular friend, who didn't even know yet that he was in a hole! I put my pen down and practiced what I'm preaching! It's so hard to remember my shepherd's crook on these trips!

If we busy ourselves counting the 99, we may well feel we have no time for the odd 1 that gets away. Let another find them, we reason. Another who is more gifted in that direction or has more time than we do. We have our work cut out for us, we reason. Yet, a loving shepherd can never, ever, forget or close his mind to the possibility of finding the 1.

In John 10, the Lord Jesus teaches us that He owns the sheep. Therefore, He cares about them. He is not a "hired hand" (John 10:12). Therefore, He feels very differently about their plight. If we would shepherd effectively, then we should ask Jehovah-Ro'i for His heartbeat. The sense of ownership of our entrusted ministry is essential. If we merely feel like a hired hand—someone who is being paid to speak or to minister to people—we will run away from our responsibility to bind up the wounded, follow the stray, or rescue the lost.

The Lord tells us He owns the sheep because He has bought them; they are in fact His, and He is able to instill in us, His under shepherds, the very same service of caring concern. He also says that He has "other sheep that are not of this sheep pen" (John 10:16). Jesus never lost His love for the outcast, the sinner, and the lepers of His day. He intends for us to follow in His steps.

To follow Him is one thing, but to follow those who don't follow Him is altogether different. And yet, the two must go together if we would truly understand what it means to say we follow "Jehovah-Ro'i." In this tender picture (the relationship of a Shepherd with His sheep) Jehovah reveals Himself to His world as the Good Shepherd. Psalm 23 and John 10 complement each other as one explains the other and paints a vivid portrayal of the Shepherdship of Jesus.

Have we sheep been found yet? Has Jehovah-Ro'i lifted us up in His arms and brought us home rejoicing? If so, are we learning to follow the Shepherd? Do we closely follow Him, feeding on His Word, being refreshed by His Spirit, and obeying His leading? Then how are our shepherding skills developing?

All of us are leading someone! Whether it be mothers leading children, friends leading friends, or workmates leading workmates. Are we modeling Jesus, owning our ministry, carefully counting the 99 to make sure that they are safe and sound? And are we further seeking the 1, ever conscious of his or her plight, putting ourselves at risk in order to bring him or her home rejoicing? If we can answer yes to all of these things, then we can know that Jehovah-Ro'i will indeed be well pleased.

•TALKING IT OVER•

1. DISCUSS.

   5 minutes

   Why do you think the symbol of a shepherd appeals to people? Read Isaiah 53:6-7. Make a list of the things these verses tell you about:

   US (*the lost sheep*)

   JEHOVAH (*our Shepherd*)

   JESUS (*our Lamb*)

2. READ.

   10 minutes

   Read the following verses and make some notes about the shepherd and sheep symbols:
   - [ ] Psalm 78:52
   - [ ] Psalm 79:13
   - [ ] Psalm 80:1
   - [ ] Isaiah 40:11
   - [ ] Isaiah 49:9
   - [ ] Jeremiah 31:10

   Which verses did you like and why?

3. READ AND DISCUSS.

   8 minutes

   Read Luke 15:1-7. Who do you think is lost? What does lost mean? What does being found mean?

4. DISCUSS.

   7 minutes

   What steps did the shepherd have to take to find his lost sheep? Compare these to the steps we need to take to evangelize. For example, the shepherd had to believe the sheep was lost.

•PRAYING IT THROUGH•

Suggested Times

1. (On your own) Read Psalm 23 and meditate on it for a few minutes. Praise God for all His shepherding in your life. — *5 minutes*

2. (As a group) Pray for sheep you know who are: — *5 minutes*
   - ☐ Lost.
   - ☐ Far away from the Shepherd.
   - ☐ Who are close to the Shepherd but are in deep trouble.

3. (In twos) Share with a partner something you need the Shepherd to do for you. Then pray for each other. — *5 minutes*

4. (As a group) Notice that the green pastures and still waters may refer to the Word of God and prayer. List some prayer requests you would like the Shepherd to answer regarding these: — *5 minutes*
   - ☐ The Word (e.g., Be more consistent)
   - ☐ Prayer (e.g., Learn to praise Him more)

•DIGGING DEEPER•

Jehovah-Ro'i (Ps. 23)

1. Read Psalm 23. List the verbs that describe the Lord's actions. Have you known these to be true in your relationship with the Lord?

2. Explain the principle each figure of speech in Psalm 23 illustrates.

   The Lord is my Shepherd

   Green pastures

   Quiet waters

3. Record the several cause and effect relationships.

   What do each of the contrasts highlight?

4. The *NIV Study Bible* provides the following list of references to the Lord as the Shepherd of Israel. Refer to each and then briefly summarize what this title contributes to your understanding of the nature of God.

   Genesis 48:15

Psalm 28:9

Psalm 79:13

Psalm 80:1

Psalm 95:7

Psalm 100:3

Isaiah 40:11

Jeremiah 17:16

Jeremiah 31:10

Jeremiah 50:19

Ezekiel 34:11-16

5. What does "in paths of righteousness" mean? (Ps. 23:3) How could you find out?

6. Recall all the "valley of the shadow of death" experiences through which you have walked. Are you still able to say with David the words of Psalm 23:4?

Recount the pain and sorrow which filled David's life. How do you think he was able to sing these words?

7. What do the rod and staff symbolize? See a Bible dictionary for help with this question.

8. What preparations do you make when a special guest is coming to dinner? In light of these, how does Psalm 23:5 encourage you?

Name something you do to honor a guest in today's culture that is similar to anointing your guest's head with oil. Why do we do these things? What does Psalm 23:5 say to you about how God treats us?

9. How does personifying goodness and love help the reader comprehend God's nature?

Where does God's presence dwell today?

The psalmist declares that this is a condition that lasts forever. Spend time praising God for His many shepherd-like attributes and for the promise that you will live in God's presence eternally.

For Further Study
  1. Memorize Psalm 23.
  2. Read two commentaries on Psalm 23 and compare them with your own study.

•TOOL CHEST•
(A Suggested Optional Resource)

THE TREASURY OF DAVID
The Treasury of David (Baker), a three-volume collection by renowned Bible expositor C.H. Spurgeon, is a timeless work. It is filled with expositions on the Psalms, preaching/teaching aids, and illustrations to enrich and enlighten your study of the Scriptures. Practical in nature, it contains humorous quips and illustrative anecdotes you will want to remember. You may wish to line your library shelves as well with other works by this great man of the Word and prayer.

8
Jehovah-Tsidkenu

•FOOD FOR THOUGHT•

Some people feel the Old Testament is obscure. It frightens them to really think about getting into it and making sense out of the old concepts and strange stories they find there. There is, however, a couplet that says, "The New is in the Old concealed, the Old is in the New revealed." The two halves of the Bible must be seen as one book with one theme. Someone has said, "There is a red thread of redemption running from the beginning of the Book of Genesis, right through to the end of the Book of the Revelation."

That is why the study of the name **Jehovah-Tsidkenu** will take us into both parts of the Bible, for the name has to do with righteousness, revealed in the Old Testament and explained and demonstrated in the New Testament. This righteousness is the result of redemption.

Jeremiah revealed this compound name of Jehovah to Israel. Jeremiah, known as the weeping prophet, had plenty to weep about! His country was in shambles and the people wouldn't listen to God. No one likes to hear the hard facts about their sinfulness, God's righteousness, and the judgment that inevitably follows a refusal to repent.

If we were to define **righteousness**, we could use the word **rightness** to explain the biblical term. God's rightness, as opposed to man's wrongness, is a truth that most would readily accede to, until it means facing up to the reaction of a holy God to our unholiness! Then most of us would send any Jeremiah who was passing along that information on his or her way.

A religious poll taken in our city regarding people's religious beliefs included this question: "According to the life you have lived up to this moment, do you think you will go to heaven?" Over 85% of the people polled answered yes. And yet, the Bible tells us that we are not going to get to heaven on our own merits! Even the right things we do are as "filthy rags" (Isa. 64:6). This is a term used for leper's bandages. It is not, I hasten to add, that God does not appreciate the fact that we care for our aged parents, work hard for charity, or throw ourselves into church work. He does appreciate all of that. But it is never enough, because the rags of our rightnesses can never cover the huge areas of wrongness in our lives!

The Bible tells us quite clearly that God has weighed us in His balance and found us wanting or lacking (Ps. 62:9). There was a particularly evil king, whose name was Belshazzar. His father Nebuchadnezzar had been converted to Jehovah through a terrifying experience (Dan. 4). Belshazzar, however, even though he knew all about this, insisted on desecrating the holy vessels from God's temple at a particularly lewd party. In the middle of his bash, a hand, unattached to a body, appeared and wrote some words on the wall. Petrified, the king eventually called for Daniel, who was very happy to interpret the writing for him. He told the king that the words on the wall—"MENE, MENE, TEKEL, PARSIN"—meant that his kingdom and his highness were through and that he had been weighed in God's balances and found wanting! This proved to be absolutely correct, as that very night the king was killed (Dan. 5:1-30).

There is, in effect, a hand from heaven that helps us to read the writing on the wall. This writing tells us that no matter how high we pile up our good works, God's balances will never dip in our favor. We will never have enough of a weight of holiness about our characters to do it! And yet, we refuse to believe we cannot come up with the goods! Scripture tells us that "there is none righteous, not a one" (Rom. 3:10). It doesn't say, "There is none righteous except one, and that's you!"

When the prodigal son (Luke 15) took off to a far country and wasted his substance with rebellious living, he ended up in a pig sty. No one doubts he was in no fit state to live in his father's house. Something had to happen to him in order for the dirt and mire to be covered. He needed to return to his father and beg his forgiveness, which he did. It was at this point his father placed the robe of righteousness around him!

But there was another son. He had stayed by his father all this time. He had probably obeyed him, worn clean clothes, attended the synagogue every week with his family, and looked just fine on the outside. But then God doesn't look on the outside—only man does that! God looks on the heart! (1 Sam. 16:7)

This young man had a very bad attitude. He harbored hostility toward his younger brother and demonstrated a critical spirit concerning his father. He too needed his father's forgiveness. Once we have realized our great need for the robe of righteousness, then we have a choice to ask for it or not!

Jeremiah realized that the people of Israel needed to make a choice about their lives. They were in desperate need of a king like David to lead them again. Even though God had promised there would not cease to be a king to sit on David's throne, it looked as if the Davidic dynasty was a thing of the past. Jeremiah predicted that Jehovah would raise up to David a Righteous Branch, a King who would prosper and bring peace and security to Israel, who would be called "Jehovah our Righteousness" (Jer. 23:5-6).

It was probably in the reign of Judah's last king, Zedekiah, that Jeremiah's prediction was given. Zedekiah's name means "the righteousness of Jehovah!" This was ironic because Zedekiah was not a good king at all. Was he to be only a bitter reminder to Israel of what might have been? We don't know. But God did promise that this Righteous Branch that Jeremiah talked about would redeem, heal, and make right the people of God. The people had a choice. They could believe the promise and put their faith in it, or they could reject the idea. Sadly, few chose to believe.

Today we face the same problem. Few believe they need help to be holy, or that Jesus is their Jehovah-Tsidkenu. Why cry out to God for forgiveness if we feel there is little to forgive or we can simply forgive ourselves and dismiss the charges? But the fact is we *cannot* forgive ourselves. Only the One against whom we have sinned can forgive us!

Jesus is our Jehovah-Tsidkenu. He is the manifestation and provision of that righteousness of Jehovah which alone can make men acceptable to God. He is Himself the Righteous Branch, living a perfect life and dying as our substitute. He is made righteousness to us (1 Cor. 1:30). Listen to these incredible words: "God made Him who knew no sin to be sin for us, so that in Him we might become the righteousness of God" (2 Cor. 5:21). "For Christ died for sins once for all, the righteous for the unrighteous, to bring you to God. He was put to death in the body but made alive by the Spirit" (1 Peter 3:18). To sum up—His righteousness is bestowed on us as a free gift through faith (Rom. 5:16-19).

Only when we realize the enormity of our forgiveness can we ever begin to forgive others. Only when we are able to look at other people and realize that God has placed a robe of righteousness upon their shoulders as well as our own, are we able to accept and forgive them for what they have done to us. But it's hard!

A woman telling me a sad story of her childhood described how her father had abused her when she was young. As she grew up, she came to know Christ and became a missionary. Years later, her father committed his life to the Lord. To her surprise, the woman found this very difficult to accept, even though she had prayed for her father for years. She had not realized that deep down she had not really forgiven him. In other words, she was angry that God had forgiven his sins because she had not!

One night, she had a dream. She dreamed her father was standing on a stage, and the hands of God, holding the robe of righteousness, appeared above him. As the robe began to descend, she began to cry. Then she was overwhelmed with a great anger.

"It's not fair, it's not fair!" she cried out. "He didn't do it to You, he did it to me." At this point, she woke up and her husband comforted her. She told me that this was a turning point for her. She realized that any sin against man is in reality a sin against God! God had forgiven her father. He was dressed in Christ's righteousness just as she was. They had much in common now. Both were forgiven sinners with their "filthy rags" covered. And both of them would be in heaven—not because of what they had or had not done—but because of God's covering!

For Jeremiah and his people, as hopefully for you and for me, Jehovah-Tsidkenu is a precious, precious name!

•TALKING IT OVER•

1. DISCUSS IN TWO'S.
   Write down 5 things you can remember from this
   session. Then share with the whole group.

   5 minutes

2. READ AND DISCUSS.
   Read Isaiah 64:6.
   ☐ This verse claims that "all of us have become
     like one who is unclean." Do you find this
     difficult to believe? Why?
   ☐ How can we tell others about this in a way that
     doesn't put their backs up?

   5 minutes

3. SHARE.
   Which illustration in this session was most helpful
   to you:
   ☐ Balance and scales?
   ☐ Prodigal son?
   ☐ Daughter abused by father?

   10 minutes

4. READ.
   Read Luke 15:11-32. What does this teach you
   about:
   ☐ God?
   ☐ Us?
   ☐ Righteousness?

   5 minutes

5. WRITE AND SHARE.
   Write a paragraph thanking God for being your
   Jehovah-Tsidkenu. Share your paragraph with the
   group.

   5 minutes

•PRAYING IT THROUGH•

Suggested Times

---

1. (As a group) Circle the word that you are most grateful for:

   peace   forgiveness   cleansing   purity   rightness

   Praise God for your choice.

   3 minutes

---

2. (On your own) Close your eyes and think through the story of the Prodigal Son. Do you identify with either son? If so, borrow the younger son's plea for forgiveness (John 15).

   3 minutes

---

3. (As a group) Note that many people believe they will get to heaven clothed in their own righteousness. Only fervent effective prayer by God's people will bring conviction. Give yourselves to prayer:
   ☐ Spend a moment thinking of someone you know who doesn't believe he or she needs Jesus' righteousness.
   ☐ Pray that the Holy Spirit will convict that person of his or her sins.
   ☐ Pray that the person will be convinced that Christ is the answer to his or her needs.
   ☐ Pray that the person will be converted.

   10 minutes

---

4. Spend the last few minutes thanking the Lord for different aspects of the Cross of Christ.

   4 minutes

•DIGGING DEEPER•

Jehovah-Tsidkenu (Jer. 22:1–23:8)
  1. Skim Jeremiah 22:1-30 and describe the political climate of this
     time period in Jewish history.

  2. What charges are made against the rulers in Jeremiah 23?

     What evidences of these crimes do you find in Jeremiah 22?

     What punishment outlined in 22:6-30 will God deliver on them?

     How is God going to redress this situation? (Jer. 23:4)

3. Read Jeremiah 23:1-8. To whom is this prophecy directed? Who is God's flock? (23:2)

What are the words "be fruitful and increase in number" reminiscent of? (Jer. 23:3)

Contrast the shepherds of Jeremiah 23:1 with those of 23:4.

Of what is the promise in Jeremiah 23:5 reminiscent? (2 Sam. 7:12; 1 Chron. 17:12)

4. Contrast the king of Jeremiah 23:5 with those referred to in Jeremiah 22. What does this tell you about His character? How will the flock fare under His rule?

5. What does the title "Lord our Righteousness" convey in this context? There is no mention of justification. What else might this name mean?

When He comes, what will be different? (Jer. 23:7-8) How would this prophecy have encouraged those who first heard it who were scattered, driven away into exile, and destroyed?

6. What does it mean to you that Jehovah is the "Lord our Righteousness"?

For Further Study
1. Using a study help such as *The Prophets of Israel* by Leon J. Wood try to answer the following questions:
   ☐ In what century did Jeremiah prophesy?
   ☐ Name three prophets who were his contemporaries.
   ☐ Did Jeremiah serve in Judah or in Israel?
   ☐ What Jewish kings reigned during his ministry?
   ☐ What tragic catastrophe did he witness?
   ☐ For how long did he minister?
   ☐ What were the causes of the Dispersion?
2. Read chapters 1–8 (under "Part One: Prophetism") and chapter 20 ("Seventh-Century Prophets: Jeremiah") from Leon Wood's *The Prophets of Israel* (Baker).
3. Do a word study on *branch*. Report to your Bible study group next week.

•TOOL CHEST•
(A Suggested Optional Resource)

Prophets of Israel
Dr. Leon J. Wood's *Prophets of Israel* (Baker) provides an introduction to the major and minor prophets plus an introduction to prophecy. The chronological sequence helps the reader link contemporaries and their writings. This allows for a developmental understanding of pre-, mid- and postexilic history, prophecy, and theology.

9
Jehovah-Shammah

•FOOD FOR THOUGHT•

Ezekiel, writing in captivity during the time his nation was spiritually and nationally at its lowest ebb, described his vision of heaven in the very last words of his prophecy. "And the name of the city from that time on will be 'THE LORD IS THERE' " or Jehovah-Shammah (Ezek. 48:35).

The Children of Israel had been delivered from bondage in Egypt only to go into captivity in Babylon! Their spirits were broken and they had hung up their harps on a poplar tree (Ps. 137:2). They were "sung out." After all, their temple was destroyed, Jerusalem was in ruins, and only a poor, miserable remnant was left in the land! Ezekiel had proved his prophetic powers by correctly predicting the destruction of the temple and Jerusalem. When these events actually occurred, the people were duly impressed and inclined to pay close attention to anything else the fiery preacher had to say.

Now Ezekiel began to preach hope and consolation. He spoke about a restoration of the land and God's people, and most importantly, of the promise that Jehovah would be there!

The promise of Jehovah's presence was not a new lesson in itself. After all, everyone knew Jehovah had announced His present presence to Moses at the burning bush (Ex. 3:2, 14-15). In Exodus 33:7-11, Jehovah met with Moses at the door of the "tent of meeting" and spoke to him "face to face, as a man speaks with his friend."

Later, Jehovah promised to go *before* His people into Canaan and also to go *with them* as they took possession of their possessions! (Ex. 33:14-16) Moses' response to this particular assurance was, "If Your Presence does not go with us, do not send us up from here" (Ex. 33:15). As far as Moses was concerned, he wasn't moving a step until he saw the visible Presence of God moving first!

So the Israelites went ahead into Canaan and Jehovah went with them, establishing them in the land. In these days, both the tabernacle and the temple were home to His Presence (Ex. 40:34-38; 2 Chron. 7:1-3). But these things were only a shadow of the reality that was to come. The tabernacle and temple were merely pictures of heaven itself. Psalm 46 uses pictures in seeking to explain a place where Jehovah's Presence was all in all. It tells us: "There is a river whose streams make glad the city of God, the holy place where the Most High dwells. God is within her, she will not fall; God will help her at break of day" (Ps. 46:4-5).

Once we come into the New Testament, we discover that Jesus Christ of Nazareth is in fact Jehovah in human form. In other words, the promise of His present Presence has been fulfilled ideally in the historical Jesus. Paul says in Colossians 1:19 the whole fullness of God was pleased to dwell in Him. The writer of the Book of Hebrews says, "The Son is the radiance of God's glory and the exact representation of His being" (Heb. 1:3). Didn't John the Apostle exclaim, "The Word became flesh and made His dwelling among us. We have seen His glory" (John 1:14). God with us, the Immanuel of Isaiah 7:14, was truly and surely "the Child, the Son, the Mighty God, the Everlasting Father, and the Prince of Peace" of Isaiah 9:6!

In his book, *Names of God* (Moody), Nathan Stone says, "The One in the Old Testament came in occasional mysterious appearances as the Angel of Jehovah, the Angel of His Presence, the Angel of the Covenant, the Angel in whom is Jehovah's name, became in Christ both the Presence itself and the temple in whom the Presence resided so that in Him and of Him it could be said, 'Jehovah-Shammah, Jehovah is there!' "

Now it is our turn. The Acts of the Apostles tells rather of the acts of the Presence than of the acts of mere men! The Presence indwells believers and now we are living temples of God. "Don't you know that you yourselves are God's temple and that God's Spirit lives in you?" (1 Cor. 3:16) Then again we read, "What agreement is there between the temple of God and idols? For we are the temple of the living God. As God has said: 'I will live with them and walk among them, and I will be their God, and they will be My people' " (2 Cor. 6:16). Jesus promised His abiding Presence to His Church: "And surely I am with you always, to the very end of the age" (Matt. 28:20).

Some who interpret Ezekiel's heavenly vision see a restored Israel's Palestine where Jehovah dwells. Others do not consider these prophecies as occurring on earth at all. But both these schools of thought would agree that the name **Jehovah-Shammah** has a final and eternal fulfillment in heaven. Jesus, praying for us in the Upper Room just before His death asked His Father that "those You have given Me to be with Me where I am, and to see My glory" (John 17:24). It is to this final and glorious end we look.

There is the pleasure of His Presence yet to be enjoyed that can hardly be comprehended down here on earth. The psalmist says, "Therefore my heart is glad and my tongue rejoices; my body also will rest secure. . . . You have made known to me the path of life; You will fill me with joy in Your presence, with eternal pleasures at Your right hand" (Ps. 16:9, 11). It is in the heavenly Jerusalem that the realization of these promises find their final joy. There we will find no temple, no outward symbols of His Presence, because "the Lord God Almighty and the Lamb are its temple" (Rev. 21:22).

> When we stand before His throne,
> Dressed in beauty not our own;
> When we gaze at Christ in glory,
> Looking on life's finished story,
> Then, Lord, will we fully know
> Not till then how much we owe!

Jehovah-Shammah! The Lord is there. Then we will know who He is. In vivid reality we will comprehend what it really means that He is Jehovah-Jireh (our substitute) and Jehovah-Rophe (the One who promises us His healing Presence). When we are there we will experience no more pain, sickness, or death! He is Jehovah-Meqaddish, our holiness, and "when He appears, we shall be like Him" (1 John 3:2). He will be Jehovah-Shalom, our peace and security. There will be no crime or muggings in heaven! It will be completely safe to go out at night because there will be in fact "no night there"! (Rev. 21:25) There will be no more wars or even rumors of war, no more personal relational wars and, therefore, no personal guilt. Jehovah-Ro'i will lead His sheep to living fountains of water and satisfy their souls! (Ps. 23:2)

Conversely, those who refuse His Presence here and now, rejecting the Lamb provided by Jehovah, will live forever under His hot displeasure, in a place that can best be described as "the place the Lord isn't!" There will be no Jehovah-Tsidkenu to hide the filthy rags of characters without Christ, no healing leaves of medicine to vanquish pain and death, no blessed injections, no sleeping pills, alcohol, or drugs to drown their sorrows. There will be no one to wipe their brow, or hold their hand as they die an endless death. People will be packed in tight against terrible hatred, insane anger, and uncontrollable sexual appetites, eternal hungers, unrestrained, unsatisfied, looking for victims. Imagine being mauled or abused in this way, or worse finding yourself perpetrating perversions and all forms of deviant, filthy, eternal sexual abuse. There will be no peace of life and limb, no peace of soul or mind, because Jehovah-Shalom is terribly absent! There will be no sign of loving. No Shepherd Jehovah-Ro'i to protect from such demonic wolves, ravening lions, or crushing bears.

To live eternally in wet shadows of sorrow, drenched with despair, huddled in a trash pit where mean memories crawl like maggots into our minds, refusing to do anything but breed a brand of tortured thoughts that chase us endlessly into searing guilt and pain until the smoke of our torment rises forever, is to glimpse a tiny bit of what it must be like where "God is not"!

Perhaps those pictures are too farfetched for some of us. Maybe the worst thing of all will be to simply see heaven from hell and know we'll never be able to reach it! No wonder the writer of the Book of Revelation tells us that now is the time to repent and turn to God before it is too late! Jehovah is calling us home—to His home! Listen! "The Spirit and the bride say, 'Come!' And let him who hears say, 'Come!' Whoever is thirsty, let him come; and whoever wishes, let him take the free gift of the water of life" (Rev. 22:17).

Where would we rather spend eternity? Where Jehovah **is,** or where Jehovah **is not?** The frightening choice is ours. Why not say, "But as for me and my household, we will serve the LORD" (Josh. 24:15). If that is our decision, we can know that one day we will see the Lord where all the full meaning and beauty of all His names will be revealed to us. Then and only then will His wonderful nature finally and fully be understood and enjoyed forever! Hallelujah.

•TALKING IT OVER•

1. DISCUSS.   *10 minutes*
   - ☐ What do you think was the most special part of Adam and Eve's day, before the Fall? (Gen. 3:8)
   - ☐ What caused "the Presence" grief? (Gen. 3:8-12)
   - ☐ Considering the above, what **should** be the most special part of our day?
   - ☐ What causes "the Presence" grief today?

2. READ AND DISCUSS.   *5 minutes*
   Read the following verses and talk about the sort of things Jesus needs to drive out of our temples.
   - ☐ John 2:12-17
   - ☐ 1 Corinthians 3:16

3. READ AND SHARE.   *10 minutes*
   - ☐ Read Revelation 21:1-4, 22; 22:6. What aspect of His Presence thrills you?
   - ☐ Read Revelation 20:10-15. What corresponding aspect of His absence horrified you?

4. WRITE AND DISCUSS.   *5 minutes*
   Write words under each of the following headings to describe what you think heaven and hell are like. Then discuss.

   Heaven   **Hell**

•PRAYING IT THROUGH•

Suggested Times

1. (As a group) Read Revelation 22:3-5 and picture heaven in your mind. Praise Him for what you see and for being Jehovah-Shammah. Picture hell in your mind. Then read Revelation 20:11-15. Praise Him for saving you.

8 minutes

2. (On your own) Think through the things you have done today. Can you think of any sin that has caused the "cloud" of His Presence to depart? Ask God to forgive and cleanse you for that sin. Thank Him for restoring the consciousness of His Presence.

6 minutes

3. (As a group) Pray for:
   □ Those who have arrogantly decided they won't be in heaven, that they may change their minds.
   □ Those who suffer the pain of His Presence through ignorance, when they could be enjoying the joy of His Presence.
   □ God to raise up missionaries to warn people of their eternal danger.
   □ Pastors to faithfully preach the Gospel to church people who mistakenly believe they are safe.
   □ Children of Christian parents who are trusting they will be all right because of their parents' faith.

6 minutes

•DIGGING DEEPER•

Jehovah-Shammah (Rev. 21:1-8)
  1. Read Revelation 21:1-8. What key words or phrases are repeated? What does this indicate to you?

Where will the New Jerusalem be located? Where will Christians spend eternity?

What will be physically different in regard to the new earth contrasted with the old?

Describe the New Jerusalem. Why is this description appropriate for the presence of God?

Compare where God's presence dwells now with where it will dwell in the future.

  2. Define reconciliation. How does verse 3 complete our redemption?

What Old Testament promises would Jewish Christians be aware of that the words of verse 3 fulfilled?

3. What will not be a part of our experience on the new earth? Which of these means the most to you and why? Pause and thank the Lord for this coming miracle.

4. Besides heaven and earth, what else will be renewed with the consummation of redemption? Provide scriptural support for your reply.

5. What is the emphasis upon in verse 5?

Whose voice is speaking in verses 3-8?

To what does "It is done" refer? How could you find out?

6. What does God's self-designation as the Alpha and Omega contribute to the message of this passage?

What do the thirsty desire?

7. Do you believe God's presence is available to you without any personal cost?

8. How can we attain all that is described in verses 1-6? What must we overcome according to the context? How does one overcome?

9. What will happen to those guilty of the vices in verse 8?

10. Praise Jehovah-Shammah for His presence. Ask for His enablement to be an overcomer. Intercede for those you know who need to know God's presence and power.

For Further Study
1. Review your lessons and memory work for all nine chapters.
2. Complete a chart of what you have learned.

Reference	Name of God	Meaning	Significance to You

•TOOL CHEST•
(A Suggested Optional Resource)

COMMENTARIES ON REVELATION
Commentaries should be the final resources for Bible study. These should be consulted only after the student has completed his own inductive study of the passage with the help of reference tools. Familiarize yourself with the theological persuasion of each commentator and compare at least two or three when you study a passage of Scripture. Determine which has the soundest arguments and the closest natural interpretation. A few for your consideration are listed.

> *The Revelation of Saint John* by Leon Morris (Tyndale New Testament Commentary, Eerdmans)
> *The Book of Revelation (NICNT)* by Robert H. Mounce (Eerdmans)
> *Revelation (NCBC)* by George Beasley-Murray (Eerdmans)
> *A Commentary on Revelation of John* by George Eldon Ladd (Eerdmans)